ADDITIONAL BOOKS B

1000 Best Wedding Bargains

1000 Best Secrets for Your Perfect Wedding

The Bride's Diplomacy Guide

The Bride's Gratitude Journal

The Bridesmaid Handbook

The Busy Bride's Essential Wedding Checklists

The Complete Outdoor Wedding Planner

The Essential Guide to Wedding Etiquette

The Groom's Guide

How to Have a Fabulous Wedding for $10,000 or Less

How to Plan an Elegant Wedding in 6 Months or Less

Love Bets

It's My Wedding Too: A Novel

It's Not My Wedding (But I'm in Charge): A Novel

The Mother of the Bride Book

Mother of the Groom

Renewing Your Wedding Vows

The Ultimate Bridal Shower Idea Book

The Ultimate Wedding Registry Workbook

What's Your Bridal Style? (coauthor)

Your Day, Your Way: The Essential Handbook for the 21st-Century Bride (coauthor)

Your Special Wedding Toasts

Your Special Wedding Vows

The Bride's
SURVIVAL GUIDE

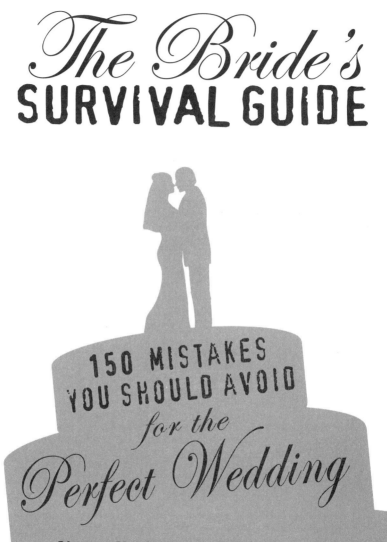

The Bride's
SURVIVAL GUIDE

150 MISTAKES YOU SHOULD AVOID
for the
Perfect Wedding

Sharon Naylor, author of *The Bride's Diplomacy Guide*

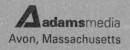

Aadamsmedia
Avon, Massachusetts

Published by
Adams Media, an F+W Media Company
57 Littlefield Street, Avon, MA 02322. U.S.A.
www.adamsmedia.com

ISBN 10: 1-59869-817-6
ISBN 13: 978-1-59869-817-6

Printed in the United States of America.

J I H G F E D C B A

Library of Congress Cataloging-in-Publication Data
is available from the publisher.

This publication is designed to provide accurate and authoritative information with regard to the subject matter covered. It is sold with the understanding that the publisher is not engaged in rendering legal, accounting, or other
professional advice. If legal advice or other expert assistance is required, the
services of a competent professional person should be sought.
—From a *Declaration of Principles* jointly adopted by a Committee of the
American Bar Association and a Committee of Publishers and Associations

Many of the designations used by manufacturers and sellers to distinguish
their product are claimed as trademarks. Where those designations appear in
this book and Adams Media was aware of a trademark claim, the designations
have been printed with initial capital letters.

This book is available at quantity discounts for bulk purchases.
For information, please call 1-800-289-0963.

CONTENTS

PART ONE.
Before You Write Your First Check 1

Chapter 1. The First Steps 3

Chapter 2. Size, Style, and Season 21

Chapter 3. The Timing of Your Day   43

Chapter 4. Speaking Too Soon   51

Chapter 8. Your Bridal Party   93

PART TWO.
The Fun Begins 105

Chapter 15. Flowers and Décor   169

Chapter 16. Invitations   177

Chapter 17. Transportation and Lodging   181

Chapter 18. Favors and Gifts   187

Chapter 19. Wedding-Day Beauty and Comfort   193

Chapter 20. Bonus Chapter!
Mistakes to Avoid During the Celebration   209

ACKNOWLEDGMENTS

With many, many thanks to my fabulous editor Katrina Schroeder and the entire team at Adams Media, my agent Meredith Bernstein, my webmaster Mike Napolitan, the many wedding experts and luminaries with whom I have the pleasure of working, and the millions of brides and grooms who have honored me by including me in their wedding plans over the years. And of course, with thanks to my family and my husband Joe.

INTRODUCTION

"I want the wedding to be perfect."

*I*t's the ultimate wedding dream, the perfect wedding day where every detail comes to life just as you planned it—if not better. The weather is gorgeous, the reception is the party of the century with delectable food and a dance floor that's packed for every song. Everyone has a fabulous time, and you've never looked better in your life. Planning your wedding is the process by which you *get* to this perfect dream day, and every decision you make takes you one step closer to the lovely image you both have in your minds.

There are a lot of steps to take along the way, and most wedding couples worry about one thing: *What if we make a mistake?* One wrong decision, one bad vendor, and it all disappears. The pressure can be hard to bear sometimes, and that can take all the fun out of what's supposed to be a joyous time in your life. Add in the fact that your parents and bridal party members worry about making mistakes too, and your wedding could become a minefield of worries. That's exactly what we're going to prevent with this book.

I'm going to alert you to the most common wedding-planning and wedding-day mistakes so that you don't get blindsided by them, so that you preempt any wrong moves before anything gets ruined for your big day. You're going to be surprised by some of the entries in this book. They're things you never would have thought about before, but they're the top misjudgments that *other* brides and grooms have stumbled over. You're going to find out which are the minor mistakes that can be easily remedied, and which are all-out disasters.

You may not have a lot of experience in all of the different industries of wedding planning—like photography, videography, floral design, catering—and to pull off a beautiful wedding, you have to become an instant expert in all of them! Who wouldn't be nervous about making a mistake? And when it comes to the *people* around you, including those already worried parents and best friends and siblings and guests, one wrong move at the start of the process and you're in the middle of a huge drama that can turn into lasting resentments—all over one comment or e-mail that was taken the wrong way. Weddings magnify everyone's emotions, so there are a *lot* of mistakes that have to do with the people around you. (See my book *The Bride's Diplomacy Guide* for handling the problems that *other* people cause. When they mess up, you can clean it up wisely!)

And *money?* Some mistakes can cost you thousands of dollars.

You have all the inside secrets right here, so you will be prepared and you will know what *not* to do every step of the way. You have the lessons from countless brides and grooms who *did* make these mistakes in the past, so this gives you a huge advantage and much better odds of having that ideal wedding day. You might not be able to prevent every thing that could go differently than you planned, but with this book you're going to learn to prevent 150 of the most common wedding errors that you can control. And then, having done so much right, you'll be a more relaxed bride and groom, enjoying the process to the fullest. So take notes, turn down the corners of pages, share the advice in this book with your bridal party and parents, and get ready to save your own wedding!

The following icons will show you the intensity of each potential mistake:

⊘ = **Minor Misstep:** It's just a little misstep that no one is going to take seriously, and can be laughed off with a self-deprecating "What was I thinking? Sorry about that!"

⊘⊘ = **Moderate Mistake:** This one's going to take a little bit of damage control, and maybe a few extra fixes to your plans—but it's not the end of the world. You may get some raised eyebrows from others who know you flubbed, but you can ignore the critiques and just go about fixing the error.

⊘⊘⊘ = **Major Catastrophe:** Uh oh, this one is *bad*. Whatever's been done or said cannot be undone. You can't un-insult someone or turn back time and do it differently, as much as you'd like to. If it's a people-centered mistake, apologize right away and send a little note of regret. It's *never* the right move to ignore a truly egregious mistake and hope the other person gets over it. If it's a potentially wedding-wrecking mistake, like forgetting to pay the deposit for your photographer and then losing his services with just a few weeks left until the wedding, get on that phone and do everything you can to come up with a new plan. This type of mistake is likely to cost you a lot of money, but the only remedy is to go to extra lengths to fix whatever's gone wrong. Just focus on the task and don't spend too much time beating yourself up. Everyone makes mistakes, and everyone has the power to make it as right as possible looking forward.

$ = **Major Money-Waster:** This mistake is going to cost you a *fortune*.

Part One

BEFORE YOU WRITE YOUR FIRST CHECK ...

*I*deally, you're reading this book before you've made any wedding plans at all. You're starting fresh with your mind full of ideas, still celebrating the newly minted bliss of your engagement. You haven't taken step one yet.

But don't worry if you *have* made some plans. If you've started chatting about the wedding to everyone you know, your parents have already started suggesting their ideas for the wedding, some vendors are booked, and guests are asking if their kids will be able to attend—you're still in great shape to prevent wedding mistakes! It's never too late to start using the insights in this book to protect your wedding dream. So read through this section even if you're immersed in your planning process, since you will still be able to use the advice and you may find that you've already done a ton of things right!

A big portion of avoiding wedding mistakes is keeping your perspective, not letting the emotions of the wedding run away with you, not making knee-jerk decisions, and congratulating yourselves for all the things you're doing well. It's the only way to keep making those smart moves and decisions, and you'll feel more confident when the later-stages of wedding stress intensify, you're getting more outside input, your vendors are throwing ideas at you, some things you want are not possible, and the wedding starts approaching quickly.

So no matter where you are in the wedding plans, the following advice applies to you. . . .

CHAPTER 1

THE FIRST STEPS

*A*ny mistakes you make at the beginning of your wedding planning, both with the details and with the people you'll work with, will last a *long* time, and they might even ruin the plans you'd like to make in the future. So pay close attention to the entries in this chapter to make sure you give yourselves the best, most problem-free start to your fantastic wedding planning process.

1. Rushing into the wedding plans ◌◌

You've *just* gotten engaged, and you're going completely wild with the planning, sometimes before the sun has set on your first day of engaged bliss. Your groom has been shoved aside as you run to your computer and start searching for the reception site because "it has to be done *now!*" Grooms say they get a little bit frightened when their brides explode like a shaken-up bottle of champagne with such intensity about the wedding plans that they wonder who this woman is. "Where did this insanity come from?" "Why the big rush, and can I maybe have a kiss first?" "Can we call my parents and let them know we're engaged before you book our florist?" I'm exaggerating, but the pent-up, speed-demon approach to wedding planning takes all of the fun out of it. The groom gets left in the dust while you're making best friends with everyone on a wedding message board and accepting *their* congratulations before you share the news with your own inner circle in a pure form. It's like a switch is flicked, and your only thought is "I'm going to be the *bride!*" instead of "I'm marrying my best friend, and we're going to have a wonderful life together." Every newly engaged couple gets that rush of excitement about the planning to come and the dream wedding day to plan ... just let the initial thrill settle into your bones for a while and focus on sharing this time with your intended rather than springing into planning mode. There's plenty of time for that later. *Plenty* of time, even if your wedding date is less than six months away. Wedding details can come together quickly, but you'll never get this moment in time back again.

DON'T: Rush right into planning mode.

DO: Take a week or so to make it all about your relationship. The groom has been through a lot of stress and worry about the marriage proposal, so he could use a nice chunk of time that's all about romance and appreciation, some quality time spent together, and your thanks to him for doing such a great job with the proposal plan. Now and onward into the future, make some couple time a high priority.

2. Not making a priority list ⊘

Speaking of priorities, your wedding plans will come together much better if you create a priority list of the top wedding elements that you want the most. Do it now, before your parents chime in with their wedding wishes and your vendors start making suggestions. What's tops on your list? The catering? The entertainment? The flowers? Write out an actual list of the top five areas where you'll decide "how it's going to be" as a couple, *before* you bring in any partner planners like opinionated parents. Things get mucky when, say, the groom's mother goes way ahead of your plans and requests certain items on the menu or a pianist for the ceremony, and you and the groom don't have any plans of your own in place as a way to protect your vision. It's true . . . some parents know that they're getting ahead of you, so this is how they insert their own wishes into the day. Then, because you want to be nice and agreeable, you feel obligated to say yes, which often leads to your being mad about saying yes because you wanted to be nice and agreeable. See how that works?

So prevent any encroachment on your wedding plans by discussing your most important wedding elements first, and being a united front about it (more on this insight later). If parents want to suggest plans for a category that's *not* on your priority list (like the favors, for instance), then you can say a healthier "yes" without feeling bossed around. You've already established that you don't have strong feelings about the favors, so it's not a problem if they flash forward to snag a plan.

CREATE YOUR PRIORITY LIST

Enter the top five items on your wish list, so that you know where to devote your time, attention, and money:

BRIDE

_____

_____

_____

_____

_____

GROOM

_____

_____

_____

_____

_____

THINGS WE ARE WILLING TO LET OTHERS HANDLE

_____

_____

_____

_____

_____

_____

_____

_____

3. **Not researching what things cost before you make a budget or talk money with parents** ◌◌

The prices out there are going to shock you. So when it's time to talk dollars and cents with parents who will pay for part or all of the wedding, it's a pretty big mistake to operate under the assumption—or let parents operate under the assumption—that the site will charge $50 per guest when the real figure is actually closer to $150 per guest.

Having confusion at the outset of your money plans almost always leads to stress—money issues will do that to any wedding-planning group—so make sure you research what packages and products actually cost. This is a big investment of time, since you won't find prices online at most vendors' sites. You'll have to set up a phone or in-person consultation, or get price sheets at bridal shows, visit their shops and get their price packages, and so on. It's the wisest move for you to arm yourselves with the actual costs of every element of your wedding plans, knowing that in many cases what you want could cost an even higher amount. But you won't set yourselves up for frustration and fights by walking into the parents' meeting with *no* figures or outdated figures, having them promise to pay for the catering or the cake, and then springing it on them that what you want actually costs five times as much.

Parents *hate* the big-money surprise, and some parents actually jump to conclusions that you're trying to rip them off, that you "did this on purpose." Sad, but true. There are all kinds of parents out there, and if you don't have an established relationship with your future in-laws, this is *not* a good way to start off with them. So, this mistake went from your not knowing to research actual prices right to "she's trying to rip us off." That's what wedding-centric mistakes can do. They elevate insanely quickly, people get dramatic and a little bit paranoid, and you wind up in the hot seat. This applies even if you're not planning with parents. Your groom might also resent not knowing what things cost if you're planning together.

DO: Research well to get a range of detailed package explanations and prices. A good wedding coordinator will have these printouts on hand, so it might be a wise idea to bring in an expert to help with your plans. Some coordinators can be hired just to help find your sites and vendors, and they might be able to get you budget-friendly prices. They can also sit down with you and your parents to present the prices with authority.

DON'T: Ask for financial commitments from parents without knowing exactly what is expected of them.

To find out the national average costs of every wedding element from gowns to cakes to photographers, invitations, limousines, and more, visit *www.costofwedding.com*.

4. **Not having firm boundaries on what parents will do to help** ⊙⊗

You've seen the traditional etiquette lists of what the bride's family pays for and what the groom's family pays for, and you know that many wedding couples have thrown those lists out the window to custom-create their own plan. Parents might be of disparate income brackets, so the groom's family might be in a better position to pay for the reception (which they may *really* want to do), in which case it just makes sense to you that parental financial contributions should be pooled into a fund that you'll manage rather than having your parents strain at their finances while the groom's parents get a big "no" from you. You might also have a situation where your parents are extremely bossy, and their financial contribution comes with lots of strings attached (for instance, "we're paying for it, so we'll decide which band to hire").

Mixing parents and wedding plans can be a tricky situation for many couples so be sure to have a game plan of your own for them. Some parents turn into veritable kindergartners, wanting to get their own way and not afraid to go behind your backs to slip the invitation designer *their* wording demands. It's stunning and sad to see what lengths some parents will go to ... they forget that they're the parents, and the meaning of the day is your happiness. Having money, to them, means having power, and they lose sight of the fact that it's an admirable thing to have the resources to give their son or daughter the dream day the couple wants. It happens all the time.

So prevent this enormous and ever-expanding mistake (that will come up again and again and again during the wedding plans if you don't take the smart step now) by sitting down as a couple to decide *exactly* what your parents will be involved in. Who's going to get the rehearsal dinner if you're paying for the entire wedding? It wouldn't be fair to let the groom's family have it on their own if the bride's family didn't get anything to plan. Who's going to attend the cake tastings with you? The menu tastings? Who will go with you to tour potential wedding sites? List it out so that you match each family's involvement with what they'd like to do *and* what works best for you. It could be that you don't want the parents at the site tours. You know that your critical father is going to suck the fun out of the entire day, so it would just work best for you to tour on your own and avoid the question of leaving out your parents and taking your groom's parents. It gets tricky when you're dividing up tasks and invitations, but you'd be in great danger of inviting conflict by not having prethought plans for their participation. Your list might look like this:

BRIDE'S PARENTS	GROOM'S PARENTS
Cake tasting	*Cake tasting*
Floral meeting	*Floral meeting*
Reception site tour	*Ceremony site tour*
Host engagement party	*Host rehearsal dinner*
Host wedding morning breakfast	*Host morning-after wedding brunch*

5. **Not being flexible** ◌

This one is just going to make *you* miserable, and probably annoy the people around you, but it's important to avoid the mistake of rigidity. When you decide on a certain color of bridesmaid dress, for instance, and then all of your bridesmaids requests a different shade that looks better with their skin tones, it's far better to allow them the blush pink over the baby pink if that's what they want. You make a mistake by turning any little variation on your request into a big drama issue of "nobody ever listens to me!" That's what the rigidity is ... being stubborn about getting your way even if it means others will be unhappy. I'm not trying to be harsh with you, but this is one of those things that many brides sink into so slowly that they don't even realize they're doing it. With so many wedding plans, and so many people's opinions flying around, there's a real temptation to latch onto any little decree and make it the measure of how much you are valued by others. If it's early in your wedding planning, this might sound laughable to you, but read it again a few weeks before the wedding. It'll make more sense then. Some brides allow themselves to be overruled by their families so often that all it takes is one little color swatch change, and it's explosion time.

Let a little bit of that pressure go by reminding yourself to be flexible with some issues, even with changing your mind on your *own* decisions. As weeks go by, you might decide that you don't want a pianist at the ceremony. You'd rather have a guitarist. Simple. Done. But then your groom makes a comment about your constantly changing plans when you've already covered that terrain. *Here's* where flexibility becomes important to him too, so gently remind him that you're allowing yourself some flexibility with plans that haven't already been booked and deposits paid. It sounded like a good idea at the time, you can laugh. Most grooms say they don't want to go over the same topic again and again. They're linear thinkers, so to them, when you said pianist, the issue was done. You can solve this problem by telling your groom that you're just brainstorming now, so he can expect a little bit of back-and-forth on some of the ideas you've been discussing. Nothing's been signed yet, and wouldn't it sound much better to have a guitarist playing than a pianist? When you explain that you're bouncing some ideas around, you give the groom the gift of understanding what your particular planning style is. How would he know otherwise? Once he gets it that flexibility is going to be a part of the plans, that nothing you're discussing right now is set in stone, you prevent future miscommunications and comments that you might take as criticism.

You make a mistake by turning every little variation of your requests into a big drama.

6. Not being organized ⊘⊗⊘

Imagine that you've paid the caterer the first and second deposits for a whopping $5,000, and then you get a phone call from them saying that they have no record of your payments . . . so you need to pay them another $5,000 now. You have no idea where the contract is, you have no idea where the canceled check is for proof of payment, and you don't have online banking to verify that they cashed your check. And that's just one vendor who requires multiple payments made on certain dates. You don't remember what you owe the florist, or what you put down for your wedding gown. Those papers are . . . somewhere. This is a monumental mistake, because these contracts and signed order forms and receipts are the guarantees of your investments. When you lose them, a disreputable vendor can rob you blind. Hopefully, you've hired reputable vendors who would happily remind you of your paid deposits, but in any industry there are always bad apples that sneak in among the good ones. And money aside, you'd cause confusion and perhaps anger when you lose your bridesmaids' size cards, requiring them to go back to a tailor to get them taken again.

Disorganization is one of the top worst mistakes you can make with your wedding, since so much rides on your having it together, being in control of the many different trajectories of your wedding plans, knowing where you stand with each wedding vendor, and knowing how to advise all of the people who are helping you to plan your wedding. You have to be a little bit over-the-top when it comes to organization, a little bit too micromanagey, for the sake of your wedding day coming out the way you wish. If you're missing appointments because you didn't write them in your calendar, or you forget to tell your mother-in-law about the cake tastings . . . that just compounds the problem. Now you're wasting others' time and creating exclusionary situations that are going to haunt you forever. It sounds like a simple thing, but too many brides and grooms don't create a foolproof organization plan from the start, figuring that they can handle whatever comes up, but then the plans multiply and swirl into a frenzy of activity. So make your plan now, and avoid the ten different kinds of miseries that can afflict your wedding plans

DO: Set up a spreadsheet or use a great checklist to keep your tasks on track, and figure out the best receipt storage system for you. You might be the colored file folder type, with pockets for papers; or you might find it best to throw everything into one oversized shoebox. You might be techno-savvy enough to set up e-mail or text reminders of your wedding appointments and deadlines, or maybe you handle everything by writing it into the blocks of your wall calendar.

DON'T: Try to take on an organizational system that you're not already familiar with. Some wedding websites and registries have interactive wedding-planning tools that will let you upload your address book and keep track of RSVPs and seating chart assignments, but if this system is beyond your understanding or comfort level, you're going to abandon it. That's the opposite of being organized. Don't skip the organization plan because you're already into the planning stages. It's easy to find planning checklists online, so print out one or two of those and check off what you've accomplished already. Again, it's never too late to establish a smart organization plan for the hectic planning season approaching you. Another mistake to avoid: don't try to force your organization plan down your groom's throat. You may have a NASA-quality spreadsheet set up, but if he's not into maintaining it with you, he's going to resist and resent your urging him to get on board with your system. Ask him which kind of reminders he wants (maybe an e-mail the day before something is due ... *one* e-mail? A note on the refrigerator?). Brides say they get the best results when they let the grooms tell them how they'd like to be kept on track.

7. **Trying to rush through planning** ◎◎◎

The wedding doesn't have to be planned in a week. If you're a superachiever, you might look at those planning checklists as a challenge—"I can get all of this done in no time. *Just watch me.*" I'm sure you can. But what fun is that? Brides and grooms who blast their way through the plans wind up with a fully outlined wedding in no time flat, and then there's a whole lot of time with no new tasks, which leaves a big vacuum where second guessing tends to happen. That cake you thought you wanted months ago ... hmm ... maybe mocha filling would be better. The second guessing is an annoyance and a mistake that you—and the people around you—don't need. Yes, you just read about being flexible with your own plans, and that still applies. The problem arises when you've *booked* all of your experts and designs, and changing them now is going to cost you money. Speaking of money, there's also the issue of financial pacing. You put down deposits on a dozen big-ticket expenditures at the start of your planning, and you may not have registered how much the balances are going to be when they all come due a few weeks before your wedding. So take your time, plan slowly, follow those when-to-plan checklists as closely as possible, and spread out the excitement of wedding shopping and detail setting. This is a task that's best done in increments. Speed planning can also lead to your adding extra things to your wedding just because you want a burst of excitement. You're bored now. You want to add a little something extra to the buffet. You have months ahead of you where you'll hear about new trends, and you may want to add even more décor. That's a magnet for impulse shopping.

Speed planning can lead to your adding extra things to your wedding just because you want a burst of excitement.

8. Counting on others' promises ⊗⊗⊗

"But you *said* you'd pay for the reception!" Cue the tears and the storming out of the room. Maybe you're not a drama queen like this, but it can *hurt* when you spend months making plans for your wedding, *thinking* that your parents are going to foot the bill, only to find out that a bad circumstance has arisen and they can't afford what they promised. It's a heartbreaking situation for them as well, since they really wanted to be able to give you your dream day, but medical bills have piled up, a job has been lost, or some other tragedy has befallen them. Or, it might not be financial . . . it could be that a friend offered you the use of her beach house as the setting for your wedding, and now she's calling with a change of heart ("we have white carpets, and I don't think I want so many people there") or the news that they've decided to sell the house. Crushing news. It's wonderful when the people around you offer to help with the wedding, but you make a huge mistake when you take initial offers—made during the excitement of your new engagement—as firm and unbreakable promises.

Circumstances change, especially when you have a long engagement period, and those generous souls do have the right to change their minds about their own homes, cars, or time commitments. For any let down that occurs, don't let it destroy you. This is the new reality, so put all that energy toward formulating a new plan for the wedding while at the same time remembering to be supportive of anyone who's having a tough time in life. The parents whose medical bills have spiked? Step out of your bride role and be the caring daughter who can pick up their prescriptions for them. The bridesmaid who had to bow out of the bridal party because she's going to be in the middle of her medical board exams? Send her a care package for her study time. These relationships will last far past the wedding, and your kindness and understanding are the best and only way to proceed.

You make an enormous mistake that has everlasting impact when you take their news as a personal affront, think only of what they're costing you, and distance yourself or guilt trip them with a sigh, saying "well, I guess we could *rent* a shore house. Enjoy that white carpet." That story is going to get around. Again, don't slide into self-centeredness, and if your first reaction was in the realm of "how could you do this to me" then it's time for a big apology, a gift sent with a card, and anything you can do to make it up to them. Selfish reactions have a way of burrowing under the skin of people and staying there forever, coloring anything you ever do again. You might not ever be forgiven. So when someone has to break their word to you, focus more on your Plan B than on what that person could have done to deliver what they promised.

DO: Think up a Plan B before anyone pulls out of their offer. When you're looking at locations, make sure you know the cancellation and refund policy. If anything happens, would you be able to get your deposit back if you cancel more than three months before the wedding? What if they can re-book your wedding date? Would you get your whole deposit back? Look into the worst-case scenario for every wedding plan now, just in case you need it later. Know the fine print of every contract that comes in front of you. And know that every promise made to you can be taken back. Life can throw some awful stuff at anyone, and it's not an easy phone call for them to make in letting you know they can't follow through. Think empathy in these cases.

DON'T: Play the pity card by telling everyone you know about someone's broken promise. Some devious couples attempt to use these instances as currency, and while I know that you're not capable of that kind of treachery, a side effect of even innocent venting can be that a grandparent or future in-law offers more than they can afford to make it up to the two of you. That's unintentional but still very real manipulation, and the lasting side effect of that is that your in-laws will always think poorly of your parents, or your friends will always think badly of another friend. Any broken promises should stay within your discretion. No one else needs to know. Blabbing creates a hailstorm of recurrent problems in your group, and first impressions last forever. Also, don't expect miracles from someone who often promises the moon and the sun and rarely delivers. It's just the way some people are. They get all excited and promise you that they'll bake your wedding cake, and they mean to. They're thrilled for you, but you know that they can be a little bit flaky. Proceed with caution in counting on anyone with a track record for not following through. Let them make cupcakes for the wedding morning brunch or something nonessential like that. It's a big mistake to count on the untrustworthy.

Proceed with caution in counting on anyone with a track record for not following through.

CHAPTER 2

SIZE, STYLE, AND SEASON

*T*he size, style, and season of your wedding are the foundations of all your wedding plans. They determine the feel of your wedding and the scope of the details, and they greatly affect your budget. Everything you do, every little thing you plan, ties into all three of these essential issues at once. Since they're so vitally important, with so many decisions hinging on them, that means that any mistakes you make on these choices can hit you many times over. Here's how....

SIZE:

9. Going too big for the money ⊘

A 400-person guest list? Is that really necessary? One of the biggest mistakes you could ever make with your wedding is going too large. And it's not just the issue of per-person expenses at the reception hall, or a $50,000 wedding cake trimmed with edible gold leaf, or importing hundreds of thousands of Ecuadorian roses—some brides and grooms have the budget for those things. For them, with their blank-check weddings, it's just what's expected for their social status. But for the non-trust-fund bride and groom, the danger is in thinking too extravagantly and justifying it as "once in a life-time" or "the day we deserve." It really *is* just one day, and it's not worth plunging yourselves or your parents into massive debt just to plan an all-out bash that goes way above what you can realistically afford. When second or third mortgages are being taken out on a home, credit cards are sizzling, IRAs are being cashed in, or valuable heirlooms are being sold on eBay to finance a top-tier wedding, that's starting off your married life with a guaranteed "crash."

Immediately after the wedding, when guests have had just as much fun as they did at your cousin's $5,000 graduation party, you're going to experience a drain, a depression, a "what have we done" level of regret that's going to ache for years to come. The best weddings don't leave you with a financial hang-over. So instead of throwing all restraint to the wind and book-ing everything you want, satisfying your every urge, scale back the budget to arrange for elements that are more *meaningful* to you and your relationship, instead of going for image and appearance. Guests are impressed for all of five minutes when they walk into a ballroom and see enormous floral arrange-ments that cost you $1,000 apiece. They marvel at the buffet spread but find themselves too stuffed to eat dinner or des-sert. Everything comes to a point where it's just too much, and "that was so nice" is the thought they take with them . . . the same thought taken away by guests at lower-budget weddings that were planned with sentimental touches.

DO: Allow yourselves to be happy with a smaller budget, and return to the proper perspective about this day being a celebration of your relationship, not a showcase for how much you can overspend.

DON'T: Go nuts with the planning, thinking this is how weddings are done. It's actually the most intimate, smaller-scale weddings that turn out to be filled with more beauty than those with edible gold leaves on the cake. Sometimes couples want the most expensive everything, and the *taste* of those items is just not up to par. That $3,000 wedding cake? It *looks* amazing, but it tastes stale. Turns out that exorbitant cake had to be baked five days ago to give the artisans time to hand-create all those sugar-paste flowers. And don't forget that with a little bit of creativity, you can find ways to emulate the most expensive wedding effects that you see in bridal magazines for a fraction of the cost. Put your focus on the quality of each element, not the price. There's no trophy for spending the *most* on your wedding.

BETTER USES OF YOUR MONEY

Take a moment now, as a couple, to list what you could use that $50,000 for that would add more quality to your life, such as putting a down payment on a house, paying off student loans, paying off credit cards, establishing a healthy emergency fund for your living expenses, or getting better health insurance plans.

10. **Going too small for the money** ⊘⊘

Just the same, you can make a big mistake by becoming a slave to the almighty dollar, and going way too far to save money on your wedding, stressing and being miserable about any expense that arises. Self-sacrifice is not the goal here either, so don't cut down your guest list to a point where you exclude all of your friends and most of your family, share a cupcake instead of having a wedding cake, or serve just pasta and soup to your guests as a way to save money. A bare-bones wedding is going too far in the opposite direction, making it way too obvious to your guests that you set out to save as much money as possible, and—even worse—that you don't care at all about feeding them or giving them anything to enjoy. A budget wedding can be planned beautifully, and even a simple and elegant cake and punch wedding is well-received by guests when you include high-quality items. So look for ways to get more from your realistic wedding budget, and avoid the hideous message a stripped-down wedding gives to guests: We're spending almost nothing so that your wedding gifts of cash will turn us a profit. Guests *hate* it when they attend a wedding and it's a no-effort affair. Big, big mistake.

II. **Getting bossed into inviting too many guests** ⊘⊘⊘

Well, your parents really know how to play you. It's a tough thing for brides and grooms to say no to their parents' pressure, especially if the bride and groom have no healthy boundaries with their parents to begin with. A really good guilt-tripping mother can run your life for as long as you let her, and the scary, controlling father can accomplish more with one raised eyebrow than a lecture of any kind. When your parents know that they can control your decisions, they're going to boss you around with this wedding. And with the guest list.

Bossy parents aside, maybe it's not a matter of unhealthy boundaries but rather your wanting to be nice and allow your future in-laws to invite all of their colleagues and neighbors . . . because after all, this is their only child you're marrying. Or their only son. Or you're just desperate for them to like you. Whatever the reason, you're allowing parents and siblings and bridal party members to add extra people to the guest list. "We can't invite Cousin Shelly without inviting *all* of your father's cousins. That just wouldn't be right!" "If you don't invite Anne and Charlie to the wedding, we're not going to come!" "Hey, since I don't know anyone who's invited to the wedding, can I bring a friend of mine?" The requests come pouring in, and what started off as a pretty big guest list between *your* own collections of friends, family, and colleagues, turns into a massive guest list—and you don't even know a third of the guests. Expensive, yes, but the bigger issue is that it cuts away at the intimacy of your wedding when there are so many strangers in attendance. You look at the dance floor and think, "who are these people?" Are they guests of your guests, or do you have wedding crashers?

When the size of your guest list spins out of control, it takes everything else along with it. Parents, then, know that they can insert their own wishes into other areas of the wedding because you're not going to say no. Determining the guest list is one of the first tasks, after all, with size being paramount to your plans. So your solution is to work together to take a stand on parents' and others' guest list requests. Let parents know who is on your guest list. Show them that you have the family covered, and unless they spot a glaring omission of an important first cousin, for instance, the family guest list is closed. If parents want to invite some of their friends, establish a fair number of guest list spots for parents. You might tell all sets of parents that they can invite ten friends or colleagues, but that's all you have room for, since you don't want the wedding to get out of hand, or have to hold it in a cavernous ballroom that costs twice what you want to spend per guest. If parents say, "we're paying for it" then they can invite extras from a B-list. Make space the primary concern, not budget. Again, go with the intimacy issue and your unwillingness to have an enormous wedding that lacks in warmth. This is a tough one, since it may be unfamiliar for you to take a stand against your parents, but now is the time to do so.

DO: Practice what you're going to say to them. It might take a few tries to get the wording that you know would work best on them, since parents have different personal concerns. You might try "we don't want it to seem like we're inviting a ton of people so that we'll get more gifts" or "we really have our hearts set on a smaller banquet hall overlooking the ocean ... if you invite all of your office friends, we won't be able to have it there." Working on a script is just smart maneuvering.

DON'T: Be manipulated by parents saying, "we'll pay for all thirty of our extra guests, so don't worry about it." Again, remind them of the space issue. It's just not right for them to have thirty of their friends while you have to cut some of your friends off of the guest list to make your budget. Don't back down ... when you're assertive, mature, and resilient, you'll get better results. It might be after a squabble or a nice comment intended to guilt trip, but when you hold firm to your position, you will get results.

STYLE:

12. Going traditional because you feel you have to ⊘⊘

Whenever you sacrifice the style of wedding you want for what *other* people want, you're going to feel it. It's like a dull ache that says, "you're selling out." And pretty soon, you will feel torn about your wish to have a destination wedding in Antigua and "being considerate of others" by having a traditional wedding in your hometown. Your wedding is only going to happen once, your parents have certain expectations—do you really want to make everyone fly to an island? Being caught in a storm of have to, must, and should is not a fun place to be. But wouldn't it be awful to cave in, then look back on your wedding photos twenty years from now and think, "that wasn't *our* wedding?" So think about how you'll feel about your own wedding years from now, and stand up for the choice that is best for you now. Remember, too, that there are a lot of prewedding events such as bridal showers that can be done traditionally and in your hometown.

DO: Make a list of prewedding parties where your parents' traditional ideas can be put to great use, such as the rehearsal dinner, wedding weekend events, the bridal breakfast, the after-party, the morning-after breakfast. Each wedding provides multiple opportunities to entertain in a myriad of styles.

DON'T: Feel pressured to have a traditional wedding because you want your future in-laws to think you're a traditional, conventional woman. Your in-laws are going to need to get to know *you*, so feel free to show them your artsy side, your love of other cultures, your spirituality. They may be surprised to find out that you love Moroccan food, or Native American culture, or orchids. And you've just introduced some new bonding topics that can bring you together as a harmonious family. Would these topics have come up if you agreed to throw a traditional, pink-and-white, flower-strewn wedding with an ice sculpture and an orchestra? Maybe someday, but isn't it fun to learn more about each other now?

> Your in-laws are going to need to get to know you, so feel free to show them your artsy side.

13. Going too indie, creating a show and not a wedding ⊘⊘⊘

All right, I'm just going to say it: This is your wedding, not *My Super Sweet 16*. And guests do know the difference. So if you're tempted to hire the equivalent of Cirque du Soleil, arrange for a laser show, and clear the dance floor for troupes of salsa dancers, you're entering Oscar party territory. For some couples, the allure of giving guests "a show" means that their wedding will be *the* party of the year, an unforgettable extravaganza that breaks the bank but impresses all who are lucky enough to get their wristband for entry into your party . . . er, wedding. There's nothing wrong with hiring live performers or having unique entertainers. It's when you lose the wedding aspect, and the two of you are no longer a part of the event. Guests will be impressed initially, and then a level of distaste will show up with everyone saying "this is over the top." When the waiters can't get through the crowd with the hors d'oeuvres because you have the U.S. gymnastics team performing in the room, or when the site manager is popping Xanax because your fire-eaters are blowing flames just a little too high, you've gone too far with the whole production value.

DO: Insert *touches* of special performances and eye-catching décor, keeping the focus on your relationship. Smaller doses of "wow" go a lot further than pulling out all the stops.

DON'T: Go too far with themes and overblown performances that overshadow the meaning of your day.

14. Having one style for all wedding and prewedding events ⊘

Why limit yourself to just one style of celebration, such as traditional bridal with the usual entrées of chicken, London broil, and salmon, when there are so many different types of parties you can plan? If you originally considered having a beach wedding, but the logistics of permits and finding a private beach for your 200 guests were just too much, you can have an engagement party or shower at a beachside restaurant. If you really love Cajun food, but it wouldn't work with your traditional, formal reception menu, then how about turning the rehearsal dinner into a Cajun fest complete with New Orleans–style dishes and jazz? The mistake is in believing that all of your prewedding and postwedding events have to match. In fact, guests love it when you give them different styles of parties to attend, since you're filling their weekend with lots of variety. This arrangement of multiple styles is also the answer if parents push for one type of wedding over another. If they want traditional formal and you want a sophisticated dessert and champagne reception, for instance, they get their wish by planning a traditional, formal rehearsal dinner. Everyone is happy. Don't be afraid to suggest that parents use their ideas for their own parties that they're hosting. As long as their wished-for theme works for you, and isn't something outlandish, then go for it.

The mistake is in believing that all of your prewedding and postwedding events have to match.

15. Letting vendors sway your choices because "they don't work with your wedding style" ⊘⊘⊘

Most vendors are true professionals who would do anything to make your wedding fit your wishes and dreams. They'll only suggest something different if what you want isn't possible or if you're about to make a major faux pas. But every now and then, mixed in with the truly talented and ethical experts out there, the "creative genius" arises with alternatives to everything you suggest. Yes, good coordinators and florists and caterers can take your idea and make it even better, but they do so with you as a partner and never against your wishes. These *artistes*, by contrast, seem to delight in twisting and altering your every suggestion and request. "No, we can't do Cabernet-colored calla lilies because that's just a little too fall-ish for your autumn wedding. I don't do cliché." Huh? They often preface everything they say with "trust me, you're going to like my idea better." Pretty soon, you start to feel pushed around, and your original requests disappear from the drawing board, your photos tossed aside in favor of the expert's masterpiece.

When a bride and groom aren't used to being assertive, as might happen with some younger couples, and when a bride and groom get intimidated by the expensive expert they've hired (who has won awards and designed weddings at the top locations in town, been featured in magazines, had a celebrity client, or just has an elitist attitude), the wedding becomes less about the wedding couple and more about the spectacular vision the expert has. The vision that he wants to photograph and use on his website or submit to an international design competition. It's a huge, huge mistake to let this happen.

No bride and groom should ever be bossed around by an expert, or have their ideas shoved aside, their budget ignored, their theme and colors and details changed on them, and then be insulted that the expert's ideas are better, more sophisticated, classier, or any other not-so-subtle putdown that could just put you even more under the vendor's control. When a vendor tries to sway your style, just say no. They work for you.

16. **Letting your location control your style** ⊘

You can have a theme wedding at any site. I'm just preventing a regret here ... this is not one that would cause harm on the actual wedding day. When you look at your ceremony and reception site, don't limit your thinking about what can be done with each space. A formal ballroom doesn't always mean you have to do the ice sculpture thing with the formal linens in a two-tone color scheme, with your wedding cake displayed in the corner. You can transform that space into a tropical paradise with the help of a great wedding coordinator and a portion of your budget shifted to rentals, flowers in hot tropical colors instead of blush pinks and whites, and frozen daiquiris served at the bar alongside the fine wines. Don't ever look at a location with a mindset of "we have to take it the way it is." Always ask the site manager how other couples have transformed the space, and find a great team of experts to allow your site to shine in a way that's better than the blank space you started with.

DO: Look at plenty of portfolios to see what florists, lighting experts and rental agencies have done for both weddings and corporate events. These pros can turn your setting into quite the scene.

DON'T: Think that transforming the space is going to cost a fortune. Yes, you will spend an amount of money for rentals and décor, but it's all in the choices you make. You could spend

$50,000 on fabric alone, or you could use a different color of tablecloths that the site has in stock, for free. The opportunities might be in the banquet hall, hotel, or restaurant's storage room. So ask about what you could possibly use.

SEASON:

17. Choosing the stormy season ⊘⊘⊘

Hurricanes. Typhoons. Tornados. Ice and snowstorms. While it's true that a storm could happen at any time, in any season, it would be a huge mistake to plan your wedding in the stormy season for any location. This is especially true of the islands that always seem to be right in the path of a category-5 hurricane. You have every date on the calendar to consider, and while the off-season's lower rates often coincide with the stormy season, it's really gambling with your wedding day to select any day within the known stormy—or ultra-hot and sticky—season. Some wedding coordinators won't even *work* weddings during those months of dangerous weather, since it's just not worth it to risk life and limb. And with some of those storms, it *is* a matter of life and limb. So do your research if you're not familiar with a stormy season in the islands or in another country—a travel agent can fill you in wisely on the best times of year to visit any locale and the worst times of year. And wedding coordinators are also invested in giving you the best dates possible for your chosen destination.

It would be a huge mistake to plan your wedding during the stormy season for any location.

18. Planning your wedding for vacation times and holidays without giving guests enough notice ⊘

Families book their vacations and their shore or ski houses months in advance, so if you're going to choose a holiday weekend—or a weekend right in the middle of summer vacation, spring break, or winter vacation—be sure to let your guests know *way* in advance. Save-the-date cards are going out as early as a year before the wedding, just so that everyone knows not to book nonrefundable vacations at that time. It's extremely considerate of you to give early warning with a save-the-date card or e-mail, since you don't want to wreck anyone's travel plans or risk their not being able to attend your wedding. When wedding couples don't send early notice and invitations arrive eight weeks ahead of the big day, forward-planning guests aren't thrilled with the big news of your impending marriage. It can mean they're going to have to try to shuffle their vacation plans, often losing money to do so. So if you must book a holiday weekend, let your guests know as soon as possible. That could be *now*.

19. **Booking during the high-priced season** ⊘

Every budget wedding book out there strongly advises that you avoid the peak wedding months of May through September, because that's the loveliest weather time and thus the most in-demand time for weddings—which means vendors and sites charge top dollar. The peak season varies depending on where you are in the country, so check regional wedding websites to see if an expert on their message boards can inform you of the true peak season in your area. In your neck of the woods, it might be that May is still a little bit cool, so peak wedding season doesn't happen until June. When you find out the window of top-dollar prices, you might wish to steer clear. Because it isn't just the catering and the flowers that are going to cost more, it's *everything* from the wedding morning breakfast to the favors to hotel and travel expenses for your guests. Peak wedding time may also be peak tourism time in your area, so guests might even have to pay more for a cup of coffee and a sandwich. Of course, some couples love the challenge of planning a budget-friendly wedding even in peak wedding season, employing a range of smart cost-cutting measures and using their network of friends and family to find fantastic discounts and freebies for their big day. With so much strategy, it doesn't matter that it's peak season. If you have the resources and the willingness to do some of your wedding elements yourself, then peak season might not be a mistake for you at all!

COMPARE SEASONAL PRICES

Check with your contender catering halls for their prices during
different months and record them here:

JANUARY

_____

_____

_____

APRIL

_____

_____

_____

JUNE

_____

_____

_____

SEPTEMBER

_____

_____

_____

NOVEMBER

_____

_____

_____

I've included both off-peak and peak months so that you can really
see the difference in per-person charges. It can be astounding, as much
as a $200-per-person difference in some areas of the country.

20. **Choosing a rough day in the family** ⊗⊗

Before you book your wedding locations and set your wedding date in stone, check with your parents to make sure that you haven't chosen a bad day in the family's legacy, such as the anniversary of a grandparent's death, the one-year mark of a sibling's divorce, or any other rough day in the family. Now, you'll have to be careful with this, since too many opinions really knock a bunch of those calendar squares out of the running. So don't ask too many aunts and uncles for their lists of no-can-do days, since everyone has sad anniversaries in their family or circle of friends. It's only the worst of them that you're trying to avoid for your wedding day, those super-close-to-you relatives like parents, grandparents, and siblings. No one can say how many years would have to have gone by for your relatives not to be upset about a death in the family, and not to hold that day as sacred. So you should never attempt to bump them out of their grief ritual by saying "three years of sadness is enough. He never would have wanted you to grieve this long." That is a *huge* mistake, even if you have good intentions of encouraging the person to heal and claim that day as a happy occasion. Yes, Grandpa would want you to be happy on your wedding day, but maybe Grandma's pain isn't the least bit faded. You have to check, and be willing to give up a prime Saturday in June if it's just too soon.

21. Not seeing pictures of your locations in season ◌

Always, always, always ask to see recent photos of your locations in the season of your wedding. Most sites will keep albums filled with 8" × 10" photos of their recent weddings, and that's the best way to see what the landscaping is going to be like, which flowers will be in bloom, such as a sea of yellow tulips or bright red summer perennials. Look also at the backgrounds, those trees in the distance. Is it a gorgeous vista of autumn yellows, reds, and oranges? In winter, are there evergreens adding some green contrast to the all-white snowy scenery, or are the trees bare and gray spindly sticks? How is the site decorated for the winter holidays? You can tell a lot by these photos, so make sure you really take the time to flip through those photo books for great exposure to the possible setting of your wedding. And don't be surprised if this flip-through reveals natural coloring that could get you to look at a different wedding date such as a spring wedding rather than fall.

Ask to see recent photos of weddings at your location in different seasons, so that you can really view the colorings of the trees, the lighting at night, and other effects.

22. **Not asking about renovations in that season** ⊙⊘

Every wedding site needs to undergo renovations in order to stay current, upgrade their features, repave their driveways, and so on. So make sure that these renovations haven't been scheduled for the time of *your* wedding. Add this one to your list of initial questions, alongside "how many people fit into the ballroom" and "do you have insurance." If you don't ask, they're not going to volunteer the fact that half of the lobby will be blocked off by a cheesy-looking portable trellis wall or yellow caution tape, and that the gardens will be off-limits, the fountains drained, and the gazebo won't be there anymore when your wedding rolls around. Better to ask about the site's future maintenance plans than experience a disappointing scene on your wedding day.

DO: Ask the site manager to let you know if they *do* plan any renovations on your wedding weekend. They don't have to alert you, but at least you asked.

DON'T: Expect to get any kind of refund on your reception bill just because there were some parts of the garden blocked off, or half the lobby was walled off. There is usually fine print in the contract that protects the site's power to make changes or alter the traffic flow on their own grounds, so while a site manager *might* throw in a few freebies to make up for any inconvenience on the wedding day, you're probably wasting your time trying to get a big percentage of your bill waived. The fine print was in the contract you signed.

23. Not taking allergy season into consideration ◎◎

It all depends on how badly you suffer from allergies, and how effective your physician is in prescribing the right course of allergy medication or shots. But seasonal allergies can take an enormous toll on your wedding day, even if you're not having an outdoor wedding!

A SITE TO CHECK

Be considerate of guests' allergies even if you're not a sufferer yourself. Adult-onset and kids' allergies can be quite irritating, and some people even stay indoors during the early morning pollen hours and then lock themselves indoors again during the afternoon mold spore hours. It's that bad for them. So add to your website a great tool that delivers the current allergen counts for the zip code of where the wedding will be held, *www.nasal-allergies.com*. Let your guests know that they should check the allergen meters before the wedding day to determine their or their kids' courses of treatment. Remember that some guests will be flying in from out of state, so they might not be aware that your region's pollen months are different than theirs. This is something you can add to your personalized wedding website to help ensure your guests' comfort.

Some sufferers get itchy, watery, even crusty eyes, massive sinus pressure, scratchy throats, and extreme fatigue from their allergies to ragweed, mold, pollen, or tree and grass cuttings.

You want to look and feel gorgeous on your wedding day, and your groom wants to be able to breathe as well, so make sure you're paying attention to allergy season when you're about to book your wedding day. Of course, being part of nature means that allergens can't be controlled, but if you know that you're a mess during September every year, don't even think about holding your wedding at that time, no matter how nice the weather is. Some couples choose destination or beach weddings to move their entire wedding away from the kind of pollens you'd find at a garden ... with no trees around at the beach, there might not be anything disturbing in the air. It's worth checking out, perhaps to make use of that great September wedding date.

CHAPTER 3
THE TIMING OF YOUR DAY

*E*verything on your wedding day runs by a clock ... you get so much time for your cocktail hour, then you're introduced into the room as husband and wife, you dance your first dance, and so on. It might seem like you don't have to think about the procession of each event, but you do. There are a few mistakes that can be made when it comes to the timing of your day, so let's prevent the following ones for you now.

24. Not paying attention to the hours ⊘

Several of your wedding experts are being paid by the hour, like your photographer and videographer who are fulfilling a five-hour package for several thousand dollars apiece. That five hours could be a mistake, considering that you could potentially book them for a three-hour package, and just arrange to cut your cake a little bit earlier in the reception. Like right after dinner, instead of an hour and a half after dinner. Your photographer and videographer get the last of the important shots and footage, and then they can be released earlier than the very end of the event. Guests can capture the party phase of the reception with their own digital cameras and camcorders or those throwaway cameras on their tables. You've just saved a few thousand dollars just by arranging the timing of your reception with an earlier cake-cutting and bouquet presentation ritual.

25. Having too much time to kill between the ceremony and the reception ⊘⊘

Some couples don't consider this a mistake. They plan for a noon ceremony and a six o'clock reception to give them plenty of time to take postwedding photos, enjoy a relaxing toast with their bridal parties and immediate families, or even spend an hour alone together. But know that this becomes a mistake when you don't provide a place for guests to go during that six-hour time lapse. Guests get very confused about where they should hang out, if they should dress less formally for the earlier ceremony and then change into something more formal for the evening reception ("I don't want to wear a full-length gown to a noon church ceremony"), and what about babysitters? Do they have to hire them for the entire day? So if you're looking at site availabilities that would require a long time gap between the two events, think it over carefully. Make sure that guests know about an ideal lounge or sports bar where they can all spend enjoyable time together until the reception is about to start.

DO: Include information about nearby lounges or the pool at the hotel where guests can gather during the time between your ceremony and reception. This is best offered as an information slip in the invitation as well as on personalized wedding websites (which many guests may not check out at all), and include a printed reminder in the guests' welcome baskets in their hotel rooms.

DON'T: Assume guests will make it to both events. When you schedule hours between the two, many guests will skip the ceremony and just attend the reception.

Don't leave guests with no place to go during several hours' time between the ceremony and reception. Many will choose not to attend your ceremony.

26. Planning a nighttime wedding when you're on a budget

When you look at the price packages at most reception halls, you'll see that a Saturday afternoon reception is often going to cost far less than a 7 P.M. Saturday reception. Formal evening weddings command top dollar, and the difference might be as much as $100 per person. So think about the fact that you can have an *identical* formal reception at noon or 1 P.M. for a much more budget-friendly figure. And guests often drink less in the afternoon as well, so if your plan is a charge by consumption, that too can cost you far less.

DO: Think about the additional perks of having a daytime wedding: some vendors charge less for daytime affairs; also, the daytime hour might mean that you can all dress less formally than a white-tie wedding at night, which can add up to savings on your gowns, accessories, and tux rentals. Menu items might be lighter fare. Guests get the rest of the evening to themselves when the reception ends at 5 P.M. Those who have traveled can enjoy some romantic alone time in the hotel, or groups can go out for after-parties.

DON'T: Assume that you can have a daytime wedding in a house of worship on a weekend without checking far in advance. Some churches or synagogues will not perform weddings on Saturday afternoons.

27. Taking too much photo time and missing your cocktail hour ⊘⊘

Again, put someone in charge of the timing of your photo session after the ceremony. Most photographers are aware that they only have twenty minutes to get more than thirty requested family and bridal party portraits, and they do their best to snap them off as quickly as possible. The mistake lies in having a distracted bridal party and child attendants who leave the area, go to check their makeup, and in short are not *focused*. Brides and grooms who allow the chaos make a big mistake, and many have missed their entire cocktail hours due to extended photo sessions. So appoint someone to be the "bad cop" so that you don't have to yell at your bridesmaids to stay right nearby, or snap at the groomsmen who are goofing off. Parents too sometimes need to be corralled, since they'll see a relative or friend and just wander off for a quick hello that eats up precious minutes. So with a designated boss standing next to the photographer with a clipboard and an organized list of photos to capture, the entire picture-taking session becomes a smooth, seamless exercise in efficiency, you get all of your wished-for pictures, and you all get to attend the cocktail hour with plenty of time to enjoy the food you selected.

Now if the photo session is running too long just because you've written down a large selection of photos to capture, consider breaking this photo session in half, capturing bridal party photos now, and releasing parents to mingle with the guests. Then, you can gather the parents shortly into the reception, such as between the first and second courses, for portraits taken just outside of the ballroom, in the gardens or out on the terrace. There's no rule that says *all* photos have to be taken immediately after the ceremony, so if it works better for you to hold off on a percentage of them until later, then just state that as the way it's going to be. There's no need for you to miss your cocktail party. All it takes is a plan, an assertive volunteer (or a wedding coordinator), and someone who's watching the clock.

> Limit the length of your photo-taking session so that you and your bridal party do not miss the cocktail hour. You can arrange for additional photo sessions during the reception dancing hours.

28. Planning to do too much yourselves right before the wedding ⊘⊗⊘

Brides and grooms who make this mistake start off with good intentions, thinking "we'll save a lot of money if we do everything ourselves." And then there are those who don't trust anyone else to handle the wedding details the perfect way they would. So they plan to do *everything* themselves right before the wedding. With twenty-four hours to go, they find themselves with a cell phone ringing like wild, ironing tablecloths until 3 A.M., still making favors, getting in a fight, and having to leave the ceremony décor setup until tomorrow morning at 5 A.M., before the breakfast and the beauty salon appointment. They may have shaved $1,000 off of their wedding budget, but they've also shaved a few years off of their lives with all that stress. So honor and respect your own timing needs for right before the wedding by bringing in either a wedding coordinator to oversee setup and do that ironing, or trust your plans to a team of reliable and responsible volunteers who can deliver the favors to your site and supervise the tent setup on the morning of the wedding. During this timetable, with your team working well for you, you can relax and get your hair and makeup done in peace, spend some quality time with your family and bridal party, and take photos at a leisurely pace before you have to depart for the ceremony. It's not worth the savings of money to run yourself ragged right before the wedding. Your time is valuable too.

WHO CAN HELP?

NAME   TASK

_____

_____

_____

_____

_____

_____

_____

_____

_____

_____

_____

_____

DO: Select several volunteers you know you can trust, and give them exact instructions such as how many chairs are supposed to be delivered to the ceremony site and what time the florist should be arriving on the scene. Make sure they have your cell phone number for emergencies, and—better yet—your wedding coordinator's cell phone number so that she can take care of the bigger problems that might arise that morning. It could be a bigger stress if all of your volunteers are calling you with emergencies that you can't handle from where you are.

DON'T: Let parents or bridal party members be those volunteers, since you'll need them with you for prewedding photos and salon appointments, plus helping you get dressed. It will turn out to be a big mistake if you obligate them to run themselves ragged while you're off getting a massage and a manicure. They'll be steaming when they return from all of their tasks.

CHAPTER 4

SPEAKING TOO SOON

Unbridled excitement is the key to the mistakes in this chapter. With your engagement newly minted—perhaps it occurred just hours ago—you're making promises left and right, in a bliss bubble where anything is possible ... or so you think. It's the equivalent of drunk dialing—you spoke while you weren't in a proper frame of mind, without thinking about the repercussions down the road. Okay, maybe it's not the same as drunk dialing, but you get the picture. What you say, people believe. It comes back to haunt you. Prevent the tricky tap dancing that almost always comes after making promises you can't keep by avoiding the following mistakes.

29. Inviting people to be in your bridal party before you've really thought about it ⊗⊗⊗

This is a big one, since your friends and family take being named to your bridal party *very* seriously. If you meet up with your friends an hour after getting engaged, and in the middle of all the hugs and screams and a half dozen toasts, you blurt out, "I want you all to be my bridesmaids!" you've just created a bridal party of twenty. On your side alone. You simply can't extend that invitation without a ripple effect. We'll get more into the mistakes of bridal party invitations in a later chapter ... for now, we'll start with the smaller issue of speaking too soon and promising bridal party spots before you sit down with your groom and figure out how many men he wants to stand up on his side. It wouldn't be fair for him to find out he now has to dig up six extra groomsmen because you invited six more of your friends to be in the bridal party. This is one of the first arguments that brides and grooms have over their wedding plans; it's even more prevalent than money issues, since it opens up a huge can of worms in the form of "don't make promises without talking to me first." And any groom who says this is perfectly within his rights! This simple mistake can introduce a massive issue in your relationship, namely being "too bossy" or "inconsiderate of what I want." Ouch!

DO: Wait until the engagement buzz wears off before you seriously consider who will be in your bridal party. Think about your honor attendants first, and then create the rest of your list knowing that you *don't* have to have an even number of men and women on both sides of the aisle. If you have two more bridesmaids than he has groomsmen, he doesn't need to find two more friends to even it out. It's a secondary mistake to pressure the groom to ask men with whom he's not particularly close just to give your photos balance.

DON'T: Say "I was just kidding" if you need to uninvite someone into the bridal party because you spoke too soon. Be honest with this horrendously difficult task. Say that you spoke too soon, and if you had everyone you wanted in the bridal party it would be a fifty-person list. So you had to make some difficult decisions, and you hope they're not upset with you. They will be, so be prepared for some major apologies and making it up to them.

Wait until the engagement buzz wears off before you seriously consider who will be in your bridal party.

30. Saying "we'll pay for your room" ⊘

It's a lovely thought, and a great gift for your bridal party, but when you make this promise at the start of your wedding plans—before all those extra charges add up—you could wind up cringing months later when you have to shell out $150 or more for each hotel room . . . especially if your bridal party has grown to a larger size than you originally thought. Plus, *word gets out*. Other friends hear that you're footing the bill for your friends, and they want you to pay for their rooms, too. (It's insanely rude of them to ask, but it does happen.) So take your time with this offer, really see where you are as far as money for the wedding, and then you can tell your bridal party members right before the wedding that their money is no good at the hotel . . . you're paying for their rooms as their thank-you gift. And if you do find that money is too tight, you can offer to pay for their rooms on the night of the wedding only, not the whole weekend. Or just get them really nice bridal party gifts in a more moderate price range.

31. Promising parents what they can plan before you have it all thought out ⊘⊘⊘

Again, your excitement can get the better of you, and you might find yourself telling the parents that they can handle the wedding cake or invite whomever they'd like to the wedding. Hold on a sec! Their enthusiasm is contagious, but you should promise them now that, "we'll get back to you on what the planning is going to be like . . . right now we just want to celebrate with you!" Works every time. Don't hand out tasks right away. There may be a money discussion to be had first, and you might find that it's better for your groom that the two of you plan every element as a duo, instead of inviting so many extra opinions. That revelation often occurs once you start talking wedding details.

Wait before you invite the parents to participate in planning the wedding. Once the engagement is announced, you may find that one or several parents transform into overly opinionated mode. You don't want to be locked into any promises when you see *that* transformation occur!

32. Booking things too soon ⊘⊘

"We got a great deal on the place! For $100 less per person than all the other places near here, we can have a beautiful formal wedding!" Yes, that offer sounds fantastic, but you haven't had time to discover that there are equally well-priced packages at banquet halls that are even better than this one. This mistake ties into rushing into the planning, so take your time before you tell vendors that they're hired. Promise yourself that you'll check out at least five different vendors in every category before you tell one they're hired.

33. Sending a save-the-date card for no reason ⊘⊘⊘

At the start of your engagement, you're going be thinking big. Three hundred guests. A horse and carriage entrance. An orchestra. A Vera Wang gown. And in your euphoric, newly engaged bliss, you might create a big guest list including everyone you and your family have ever known. Since save-the-date cards are now *the* way to let people know where you're registered for gifts (wink, wink), these are going out a year in advance ("Hey, they have to make their travel plans and book their hotel rooms, right!"). Now here's the danger: if you send out save-the-date cards to your 200 guests, before the parents and the groom make their lists, you *have* to invite these people to the wedding. There's no cutting down the guest list after this. They've been told to save the date, so they expect to be invited to the wedding. Some cancel their vacation plans. Some book their flights right away. Some don't register their kids for summer camps. It's a *huge* mistake to not send an invitation to those who got a save-the-date card, so hold off on these announcements until you see some prices and put down some deposits, to really get a look at your true wedding budget. And that goes double if you're buying a house or getting a bigger apartment together . . . home expenses add up.

DO: *Wait* until you know what you're doing before you send your save-the-date cards. They really don't have to go out until nine months before the wedding, but they should go out sooner if your wedding will be during vacation or holiday time. This means you need to step up your planning to get a feel for the size and scope you can handle.

DON'T: Send them out, and then send "so sorry we can't invite you after all" e-mails to all the people you cut from your guest list. Sounds like a considerate idea, but it's really just going to insult everyone.

34. Announcing a destination wedding, and then changing your mind ⊗⊗⊗

You would be surprised how often this happens in our current world where the destination wedding is all the rage, resorts offer incredible packages including free honeymoon weeks, and smaller groups of guests make planning easy. But when that smaller group of guests make their travel and hotel reservations for your destination wedding, and then you announce that you've changed your mind and are having a hometown wedding, they may lose money on their airfare and lodging … and be *very* angry with you. You become known as the flaky bride, and they resent the time they spent in line at a government agency applying for passports. So to prevent this extremely heinous wedding mistake, never announce your plans for a destination wedding unless you're fully committed to it, plans are in motion, you've paid a deposit, and you're already working with the on-site coordinator.

KEEP THE PLANS HUSH HUSH

For *any* wedding plans, it's often best not to talk too much with others about your ideas and visions for the big day. As you progress into the planning stage, and into your credit card balance and savings account, you may find that some of your ideas aren't possible. It would be a big mistake to continue on with plans you can't afford just because you promised everyone certain elements to the day.

CHAPTER 5

LISTENING TO OTHERS

*E*veryone has an opinion. You're going to hear so many of them, it can take the fun out of the planning, or pressure you into making choices you wouldn't otherwise have made. When it comes to your wedding, agree to listen to others' opinions and thank them for sharing, but still make your own choices. You're going to hear a lot of "but that's how it's done" from parents, recently married friends, people on bridal message boards, and vendors, and the mistake is agreeing to be controlled by public opinion. Yes, there's some insight you'll receive that will help you save money or avoid an etiquette flub, but the mistakes happen in the more planning-centric aspect of it, when others press you to include certain songs or readings in your ceremony, or to have your wedding in a house of worship when that's not your first choice.

GET AN EXPERT'S ADVICE

Weddings turn everyone into experts, at least in their own minds, so here's an inside tip: You can *write* to an expert (that would be me) with your questions about what's proper and what's not proper. Visit me at *www.sharonnaylor.net* to see if what's being thrown at you really *is* how weddings are done.

35. **Giving in to parental pressure** ⊘⊘⊘

Most parents don't mean to be bossy or controlling. Something takes them over and they become *very* invested in the wedding, often losing sight of the fact that it's not their day. So when they start pushing for just one little thing their way, one change to your stated plans—a few tweaks to the menu here, a few songs added to the playlist there—you need to put your foot down. Gently, but now. It's a huge mistake to let parents get away with the first few pressure tactics, because they're going to start piling even more requests on soon. So come up with a tag-team line that you'll use to put some distance between the parent's smoothly worded request and your answer, as in "hmmm, a groom's cake? Let me talk to [groom] and see what he thinks about that." You're not putting it all on him, of course. Scapegoating your future spouse is an even bigger mistake. You're just buying some time to let the request hover in the air, and then you'll call back with a businesslike "we talked about it, and we really don't want any more desserts than we have. Thanks for the suggestion, though. Maybe you can include that in the rehearsal dinner, or some other event?" You prevent a major mistake when you let them down gently, keep your united front, and suggest a replacement plan that lets them "get their way" on something without it actually affecting the wedding plans. This is an important lesson to put into place right now, since couples who have let the parental pressure get to them wind up with wedding days that are not *theirs*, that don't reflect them or their relationship or even the things they like. They got pushed around, and that hurts for a very long time. Add in the guilt about being mad at their parents when "they were only trying to make it nice," and that's a scary cocktail. So prevent future regrets and wedding day disappointment by having a plan to just say no to parental pressures.

It's a huge mistake to let parents get away with the first few pressure tactics.

36. Competing with other brides and grooms ⊘⊘

If there are a lot of other weddings in your circle of friends or within your family, there's often a pull toward wondering how your wedding is going to stack up to theirs. "What if our wedding looks cheap compared to Cousin Sally's country club wedding?" Many mistakes have been made when brides and grooms try to compete against other weddings, inflating their plans and their budgets in trying to make a bigger and better impression. So don't invite this mindset by grilling your friends about their wedding plans. Be happy and excited for them if they start talking about their invitations or their gown, but don't get into the oneupsmanship game. It's very annoying to others if you answer their every statement with a report on how *you're* doing it as well, so just be a good listener, and share details about your day if you're asked, enjoy talking about your plans among your friends, but remind yourself that every wedding is different no matter how grand or how intimate, and neither is ever better than another. What matters most is that the plans you make are significant to the two of you.

DO: Ask others questions about their weddings only to allow them the enjoyment of talking about their big day, not to pry for information.

DON'T: Ask what they're spending, or show your insecurity by saying, "wow, we couldn't afford that" or "I *wish* we could have fireworks, but my parents are being really tight with their money." Now you've just acted like a brat, blaming your parents. It's a downward spiral, really, so keep yourself clear of the competing mindset. It's not becoming to any bride.

37. Going by the wrong rules and advice that you read on a message board ⊘⊘

Message boards at bridal websites are great communities. They allow you the chance to bounce ideas off of objective third parties, vent your frustrations when you choose a really obscure screen name that your friends wouldn't recognize as you (very important!), read about creative do-it-yourself projects that would help your budget, and more. But you have to be really careful when you pose a question to any message board about something really important, like whether or not to marry in a church, or whether or not to have your bratty sister be a bridesmaid, because you're going to get a range of answers that can tend to confuse you more than educate you. Sometimes, the fewer opinions the better, because some people lurk on message boards to get a perverse thrill out of giving wrong advice, or playing devil's advocate to otherwise good advice posted to you. If you become too dependent on the advice from strangers, your own intuition can get dulled. No one who doesn't know you or the people involved in your situation can solve your problem; only you can. So don't look at message boards as free therapy, and don't run with the first posted piece of advice you get. Take everything you read under advisement, and if these responses just back up what you were going to do anyway, there's the validation you were looking for. So there is merit to belonging to a good online community, but just don't go overboard.

> **Don't look at message boards as free therapy, and don't run with the first posted piece of advice you get.**

38. Not booking because someone complained about the crabcakes ⊘

"Yeah, we went to a wedding there, and the crabcakes were terrible!" When you ask a friend what she thought of a reception hall that's on your list of possibilities, and she shares an opinion like this one, it's just a personal opinion on one dish, and not a universal judgment on the place as a whole. Maybe those were award-winning crabcakes and she just doesn't like spicy foods. And some people are negative-filter people. They *loved* 99 percent of the food at that wedding, but they're only going to talk about the crummy crabcakes. For any referrals you seek from your friends, just note what they have to say when the feedback is about one small part of their experience and keep it in mind for when you check this place out further. Now if they said, "the place was dilapidated, and we could hear the music from the wedding in the next room," that input should get a little bit more emphasis in your considerations.

DO: Take note of friends' complaints and rave reviews, knowing it's just their opinion, and see if you agree when you check it out for yourself.

DON'T: Eliminate what could be the perfect place just because one person was in a whiny mood that day and chose to focus on a small detail that wasn't to his or her pleasure. And don't base your choice of location or vendor all on one person's opinion. If you only have one recently married friend, talk with her as well as with people who have attended holiday parties and corporate meetings at the hotel ballroom. They often have great input about the quality of the food and service, for instance, since it's the same chef and often the same menu.

39. **Booking on referral without total research** ⊘⊘

Booking a place or a vendor just because someone says they're awesome is just as bad as counting out a potentially great place because of what a friend says about it. When you limit the necessary research steps, trying to get the task done in a hurry, thinking that your friend always knows the best places, you could miss out on a terrific new option that you could refer *her* to in the future. Taking others' word as gospel is a moderate mistake in that you limit the thrill of discovery and the new things you can learn during consultations with a large range of vendors. You see fewer portfolios, tour fewer sites, and absorb less inspiration this way.

CHAPTER 6

THE MONEY ISSUE

Mistakes made with money have a devastating effect on your future financial health, and since money is one of the top causes for fights in relationships, any blunders here can cause arguments with your fiancé, resentments among your parents, and high levels of stress that get you snapping at everyone around you. When you pay careful attention to the following mistakes, you'll keep the peace in your most important immediate circle and your wedding will remain all about your marriage, not all about the money.

40. Not making a budget ✗

Don't think that you can keep the numbers under control in your mind. The big purchases tend to hit a point where they all get blurred, and then when all the little purchases and additions come along, you really have no idea what you've committed yourselves to. Most couples who don't put their budgets on paper guess that they've spent 40 percent less than they actually have when asked for their current figure. Then they get the air knocked out of them when the actual tallies come in. So print out a working budget with spaces allotted for all of the major and minor expenses, and keep it handy for every step you take.

DO: Make it a strict practice to update the budget list every time you make a plan or a purchase.

DON'T: Use a spreadsheet without backing it up onto a separate disk or making regular paper printouts of it. If your computer crashes or your file is lost, you're in big trouble. So follow wise computer smarts and back that file up often.

> **DON'T LOSE YOUR DATA!**
>
> If you don't have a zip or flash drive, ask a tech-savvy friend to help you save your files to a separate location, not just to a separate file on your same computer's hard drive. Such valuable information needs to be kept in a safe place in case anything happens to your computer as a whole. So every now and then, back up your files several different ways. And don't look at paper printouts as ancient methodology. Kept in a folder as a time capsule keepsake, these records will show your kids how people planned weddings way back when.

41. Assuming parents will pay ⊗⊗⊗

You haven't spoken to either set of parents about the financing for your day, but you think, "parents always pay for weddings." Not true. Parents who know your engagement is coming are checking out bridal websites and advice columns, and they know that it's becoming a *minority* of occasions where parents foot the entire bill. Now, most parents play a supporting role in paying for the wedding, maybe splitting the bill with the bride and groom, or asking to take care of a few elements like the flowers and the cake. Brides and grooms blindside themselves when they just assume that parents will pay for the extravaganza they have in mind, and when they start making plans and getting emotionally invested in the things they want for the wedding, only to find out that parents can only give a fraction of the expected contribution. It's very upsetting. Add in the fact that parents can get offended if you just *assumed* they would pay, or if you descend into a tantrum or blame them for ruining your wedding dreams. I've heard from too many parents of the bride or groom with a heinous story, such as the bride who demanded that her parents cancel their planned vacation to Greece—"*then* you'd have money for my wedding!" She called her parents selfish, and then launched into a tirade about how they spent so much money on her younger brother's education when they *knew* they'd have a wedding to plan someday! The range of anger at parents, when a bride or groom has an unrealistic expectation about financial help, includes the silent treatment, vengefully cutting them out of the areas where they *do* want to contribute ("so there!"), and even trying to play the groom's parents against the bride's parents in a horribly manipulative game to get more wedding money. Don't count on parents' financial support for your wedding. Just be pleased with what you're offered, and use that to the best of your ability.

HOW TO ASK ABOUT PARENTS' CONTRIBUTIONS

The correct phrasing is: "How would you like to be involved?" Not: "What would you like to pay for?" *Big* difference.

42. Maxing out your credit cards ✑

Every financial health article, book, and website in the world warns against maxing out your credit cards, since it's your valuable credit rating that's on the line. If you run up massive bills, not only will you spend an enormous amount more in finance charges, but your credit rating also suffers when you carry high balances on several cards. And if you're late making payments, or if you go over your limit, that too shows up as a red flag on your credit reports at the three major agencies. This issue often escapes the attention of brides and grooms during the wedding plans, but it causes massive problems when they want to buy a house in the future. When you apply for a mortgage, the mortgage company looks at your credit rating. If it's too low, you're not going to get a good interest rate on your home loan, or you might even be denied the loan. No new house for you. It's that important to respect your credit cards. Use them for wise purchase protection for the big things, but don't go nuts with the all-out spending on extras you don't really need. Make it a high priority to pay off as much of your credit card balances as you can each month, so that you don't get stressed by growing and growing balances that arrive in the mail each month before the wedding. When even the minimums strain your checking account, you're getting into dangerous territory. So if you have to eliminate some of the more extravagant plans you wanted for your wedding, congratulate yourself for respecting your own financial strength in a fulfilling future together. When you walk into your new home, you'll be happy you didn't spend a fortune on that stretch Navigator limo for the bridal party or the first-class airfare to Nevis.

43. **Counting on cash wedding gifts** &

If you ran up your credit card bills, thinking "no problem! We have 200 wedding guests invited, and they're sure to give us at least $250 each in wedding cash, so that more than covers our credit card balances," you're in for a big shock. And a huge financial mess that will hobble you for years. Very few wedding couples are earning back their wedding expenses, since more guests are giving lower amounts of wedding cash. Some who travel to destination weddings are not giving much in the way of cash gifts at all, since they're spending so much to attend a faraway wedding. Plus, it might be tradition in your family for everyone to give cash or a check in an envelope as the wedding gift, but in many regions of the country, cultures, and families, guests bring a wrapped gift. Since we're a global society, we're experiencing the meeting of many different regional practices that come together on a wedding weekend, and that can stun a bride and groom. They expect to walk out of their reception with a sack full of cash, and they actually wind up with enough cash to pay for the photographer and videographer, plus some really great silver platters and more of their china settings. And a salad spinner.

DO: Look at cash gifts as icing. It's not money you need to get out of debt, since that's quite a gamble, but whatever you get will be of great help to all of your financial goals.

DON'T: Tell guests that you want cash contributions to pay for your new house or to pay off your student loans. That is such a big etiquette don't that guests get highly offended, and you look horrifically greedy. Some couples try to be tricky, not registering for gifts and expecting that guests will read that as a signal that they should give cash. You're only going to get an ugly vase because the guest who gives wrapped gifts had no suggestions about your style.

Don't count on guests giving you cash gifts, thinking that's how you'll pay for the wedding. Many guests give less than you would expect, some give wrapped gifts from your registry, and a sad new trend is that some guests attend weddings without giving a gift at all. It would be a huge mistake to plan a big, lavish wedding thinking you'll make all that money back in gifts.

44. **Paying with cash** $

Even though you're not supposed to max out your credit cards, you should use them wisely as a way to protect your investments. When you're putting down a deposit, use a credit card or check as a way to prove that you paid the bill. When you hand over an amount of cash, there's no transaction record, no consumer protection plan to keep you from being had by an unscrupulous vendor. So for all but the smallest purchases (like bags of chocolate for favors or other take-home items), don't pay with cash. And get a signed receipt for everything that you do book or purchase. Don't worry about seeming paranoid when you ask for a signed receipt or an initial on the contract next to the spot where it lists the deposit payments and due dates. You're just being a good bridal consumer.

45. **Not reading contracts fully** $ ⊗⊗⊗

Huge mistake! Make sure you read any vendor's contract fully, so that you know about any hidden fees, so that you understand their cancellation and refund policy, their deposit due dates, any disclaimers they have, or rules you're about to sign on for (such as, "you'll hire our caterers and our florist," "no children allowed," or "we reserve the right to cancel your wedding at any time"). Once you sign your name to a contract, you agree to *everything* in there, and it will stand up in court. So take your time in reading the contract, don't let a vendor rush you into signing by saying, "oh, it's just a standard contract like everyone else has." If you have questions, ask. Don't worry about looking silly or uninformed. A good expert knows this may be your first time dealing with special event issues. If you ask for changes to the contract, get them initialed by the vendor, and make sure you get a copy of the entire contract, not just your receipt.

AN ESSENTIAL CONTRACT CLAUSE

Make sure that your contracts contain the phrase "time is of the essence" or some similar wording that requires your vendor to deliver goods and services at a specific time, such as an hour before the ceremony start time to allow for setup. And specify that exact delivery time. An unscrupulous florist who arrives five minutes before the wedding and decorates while guests arrive *has* met the contract terms to have the place decorated for the noon ceremony, even if he or she wrecked the arrival effect you dreamed of and caused you great stress.

46. Not knowing deposit deadlines ⊘⊘

If you're late in paying, they can slap you with a 5 percent late fee. And that adds up. So be ultra-organized about when each deposit is due for every element of your wedding plans, and double-check to make sure the amounts are correct. If you're organized, you will catch a simple clerical error of your second deposit not being recorded as paid. If you're not organized and your budget is in your head, not on paper, you're going to pay that invoice twice. Record your deposit schedules here:

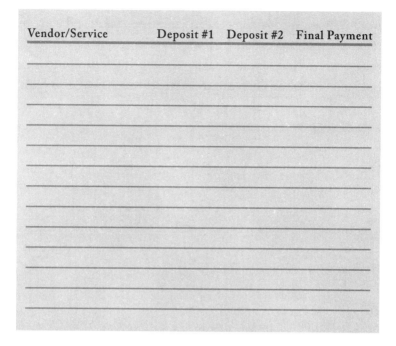

Vendor/Service	Deposit #1	Deposit #2	Final Payment

47. Allowing emotions to get away from you, spending more because this is "once in a lifetime"

Check back over your initial priority list, as well as any notes you took early on in your thought process as a reminder of what your needs are, as opposed to your wants. When emotions run high, it's those wants that pop into your mind when you're least prepared to resist. With a mindset that "this is once in a lifetime," your willpower can sometimes falter and you can make impulsive decisions that expand the scope of your wedding plans as well as your budget. Yes, this is once in a lifetime, but sometimes so is bankruptcy. Your emotions will run high, encouraging you to splurge, but take that impulse to another area of your life.

DO: Use that energy to excel at work, organize your home, create a sentimental scrapbook of your relationship for display at the wedding, or volunteer one weekend at a food bank—all acts borne of great love and gratitude. And they're far more rewarding than spending $5,000 on extra desserts you don't need at your reception's final hour.

DON'T: Appoint your fiancé or a friend as your gatekeeper, with instructions to stop you from overindulging or overspending on the wedding. You're only going to get mad at them when they gently tell you to rein it in, and that turns into an intensity-fueled fire that doubles the problem. Now, you've spent too much money and you're fighting with that close, trusted friend because you didn't want to hear the no you asked for months ago.

48. Going too far to save money ⊗⊗⊗

There's a big difference between a wedding planned on a budget and a cheap wedding. A cheap wedding shows where you cut corners, such as flimsy flowers you cut from your own garden, serving just salad at the reception, or having bad do-it-yourself projects as centerpieces. There are smart ways to save on every aspect of your wedding plans, and then there's being way too obvious that you were trying to save cash at the expense of quality. You may like the numbers on your budget spreadsheet, but when these decisions come to life on your wedding day, disappointment is certain to follow. When you don't invest wisely, you're left without essentials, with tacky décor, guests left hungry, music that stops too early, and a hem that falls on your wedding dress. This one big mistake cascades throughout every element of your day, tempting the fates to have multiple things go wrong on your wedding day.

49. **Not taking guests' expenses into consideration** ⊙⊙

You might love that mountain resort as the setting for your wedding, but if the hotel room rates are $300 a night, is that really fair to do to your guests? Should you require them to spend three times what they would have spent for a different location, just because you wanted your photos taken by that resort's indoor waterfall? This is not to say that you should choose the cheapest hotel in the state as the setting for your wedding. Just be careful that you're not overobligating your guests to spend a fortune on top of the effort it takes for them to reach wherever the wedding will take place. You're not required to pay guests' travel and lodging for a destination wedding, but some brides and grooms choose to do so. That's up to you and your budget. But for any part of your wedding weekend that will require guests to spend their money, always make sure you've chosen something in the moderate range, or at least offered them a second price range, such as a nearby resort or hotel with $100 rooms and a great swimming pool. The average number of hotel room blocks is two, with many guests opting for three.

DO: Look into budget-friendly lodging, such as bed and breakfasts.

DON'T: Make a room block of all suites. You can let guests know that they may upgrade their rooms to suites for an amount of money you've determined ahead of time; just call the hotel at the reservations number.

BED AND BREAKFASTS ON THE MENU

Find a great range of bed and breakfast establishments, some with pools or free limousine service, free beach access and free bike rentals, winery tour passes, and more at *www.BnBFinder.com*

CHAPTER 7

YOUR GUEST LIST

*M*istakes made with money are bad enough, and have a lasting impact. But mistakes made with *people*? These are often the worst category for wedding planning, since people hold a grudge, people gossip, and people remember everything about how you treat them with regard to your wedding. It's a funny thing about weddings . . . people use them as a gauge of how important they are. You might not have invited certain cousins to your graduation parties and that was no big deal. But not inviting them to your wedding? Travesty! Parents especially care about what other people think, so watch your step in this minefield of potential mistakes.

50. Verbally inviting people before your plans are set ⊘⊘⊘

Again, the excitement gets you—and your parents, who are often the major offenders with this one—and you've mentioned the wedding to the entire family before you've really even figured out your budget or your locations. Colleagues think they're invited, your parents invite their friends, and pretty soon that guests list is out of control. And then you have to handle the inevitable letdown of letting parents know that they can't invite so many of their friends, or let your colleagues know that you're out of space so while you *wish* you could invite your closest coworkers, you can invite some but not all. It turns into a mess. So here's your solution: tell your parents *now* that you're putting a gag rule on the wedding plans. They're not to invite anyone until you're at a good place in your planning, know your budget and your space availability, have your locations booked, and know just how many people can share in your big day. With the ruling handed down now, you prevent a collection of major mistakes that hurt feelings and get parents wheeling and dealing to get *their* friends invited to the wedding they're helping to pay for. Egos stay out of it, and it becomes a timing thing.

51. Not giving "and guest" invitations according to a set rule ◌◌

This one falls under the etiquette heading, and according to etiquette, every single guest over the age of eighteen should get an "and guest." Today, though, with weddings being so expensive and guest lists so large, some couples are taking etiquette into their own hands and creating their own rules for the "and guest." It could be that guests can bring a date only if they're engaged. As you might expect, that creates a firestorm of controversy. What happens to the longtime couple who's been together for five years but isn't engaged, when the cousin who just got engaged to the guy she met on the Internet two months ago qualifies for an "and guest"? This is the kind of thing that offends people, gets the gossip mill running full steam, and starts those "what about me" e-mails pouring in to you and to your mother, controversy swirling all over the place. To avoid this current firestorm, you can decide that you'll give an "and guest" to all your single guests. Include senior citizens who appreciate the gesture, and often bring their personal aides or nurses as a treat and for their own assistance. It's just a cleaner way to handle your guest list, and it prevents a ton of additional mistakes that almost always follow a "no and guest" ruling ... and those would be giving in to pressure from some guests, allowing them to bring a date, and then others hear about it, and pretty soon, you have a lot of hurt feelings. It is okay to specify that teens are not to bring dates. That one is okay to claim without controversy.

Anything other than allowing all singles to bring an "and guest" creates controversy. So think twice about making a ruling that only guests who are engaged can bring a date, since you might offend longtime couples who have been together for much longer than that impulsively engaged couple on your list.

52. Allowing some guests to bring kids after you've said "no kids" ⊘⊘

Again, this mistake taps into the mass confusion caused by your backpedaling on your own rule and giving in to pressure. Guests know that when they get a wedding invitation and it doesn't say "and family," that it means their kids aren't invited. And many guests are happy about that. A night out without their toddler? Bring it on! Of course, there are always some guests who look at your wedding like a family reunion, thinking "This would be a great opportunity for all the far-away relatives to meet my two kids for the first time!" So you get phone calls and e-mails asking if they can bring the kids, and then you'll also get the litany of issues such as not having a babysitter, not being ready to travel without the baby, and so on. Your solution to this is to let the guests know that they can bring their kids with them into town, and to the hotel, but not to the wedding. And when they call to say they heard your sister's kids are invited, because they're the flowergirls, you might be pressured to let it slide just this once. And then another time. And then you have forty kids invited, with half the guests certain to be angered over the fact that they went by the rules and hired a babysitter when so many other people weren't required to do so. It really is quite unfair, and they have every reason to be upset. When you essentially ignore those who have honored your request, it comes off as favoritism or a double standard. Which doesn't make for a happy wedding guest. Worst of all is when they find out *at the wedding* that so many others were able to bring their kids.

DO: Stick to your plans about guests bringing kids. You can allow the closest kids in your life, such as the flowergirl, the ringbearer, and your best friend's child who is your godson, and not worry about any perceived favoritism from other guests, since it's a given that you will have a few VIP kids in attendance.

DON'T: Make exceptions for anyone, and don't allow parents to pressure you into making exceptions for anyone who wants to bring the kids along. For anyone who asks, let them know that there will be plenty of mingling and social time during the wedding weekend for them to show off their kids, but for the wedding itself, would they like to hear about the special babysitting suite you've arranged with qualified babysitters and a kids' menu? Case closed!

53. Allowing parents' guest lists to take over your space ⊘⊘

If parents are paying for all or part of the wedding, they see it as their party. They may feel entitled to invite a few dozen of their closest friends, which takes valuable space away from your ability to invite all of your friends. Parents say it's important to share this big day with their friends, since their friends are all so happy for you and supportive of your happy marriage, and that their friends are likely to give more generous wedding gifts. That shouldn't matter at all. When you find yourself in a situation where your parents have more friends invited to the wedding than you do, something is wrong with this picture. Sensing your oncoming confrontation, parents step up with the dreaded "we're paying for our extra invited friends, so what's the problem?" The problem now multiplies, because they just insulted you by implying that your issue is the money. That you're greedy. Somehow, they managed to gloss right over the fact that they're hijacking your guest list and outnumbering the people with whom you're closest. So prevent this dangerous mistake by stating early how many guest spots your parents can have. If you're at any early stage of the wedding plans, tell them (in that same conversation where you say that no guests can be verbally invited yet) that you're ballparking their allowable friends guest list at fifteen for now. Once you get a more realistic feel for your own guest list, you might expand or contract that amount. If parents feel the first sting of your taking control, just lighten it up with a smile and a simple: "We just have to figure out how many people we can fit in our locations, and we don't want an enormous wedding that's more like a circus." Parents also might need to hear: "A more intimate, smaller wedding would be far more impressive to all of our guests, because we'll have more money to devote to the beautiful things like the flowers and the cake. We don't want a giant wedding that doesn't have anything beautiful, right?" You've just prevented an enormous problem by buying time now, and figuring out your parents' guest list later. *That's* the best way to avoid this mistake.

State early how many guest spots your parents can have. If they have big plans and want to invite dozens of people, suggest that they renew their vows or allow you to plan a big birthday party for them instead.

54. Giving in to friends' pressure to extend obligation invitations ✃

It's not all your parents' fault. Sometimes it's your other friends who put the pressure on to invite satellite friends and other couples with whom you all socialize. You might not have spoken with some of your college friends in years, but, they say, wouldn't it be great if you could all get together at your wedding to reconnect and relive old times? That's what class reunions are for. This is your wedding, and the only people who should be invited are the people with whom you're currently close and who you plan to have in your life in the future. If some members of your former circle of friends have drifted away, there's a good reason for that. You'll know the difference between friends who have just been busy or live far away, those who you can go six months without talking to but it's like no time has passed when you *do* call to catch up. That's not the kind of friends we're talking about here. We're talking about friends you have outgrown, or with whom you have nothing in common anymore. It's just a different feeling, a sense of dread when you think about devoting two guest spaces to them. If you're feeling *dread*, it would be a mistake to invite them. So close down the peer pressure by letting your friends know that you'll see those other friends at the class reunion someday but for right now, you're sticking with friends you talk to often and see often.

55. Expecting no friendly exes on the guest list ⊘⊘⊘

This mistake hovers between brides and grooms, without the family and friends involved, which can actually make it even more intense. Either you or your groom wants to invite an ex to the wedding, and that idea is not going over well. It doesn't matter how intense the relationship was, if it was intimate or if you never slept together, the issue is often the same. You don't want your groom to even be reminded of an ex-girlfriend on your wedding day, and wouldn't seeing her there automatically bring up memories of their vacation to Mexico? It's an insecurity roller coaster if you let yourself get caught up in petty jealousies over a friendly ex on the guest list when the ex in question is out of the picture fully. If she's married now with three kids, and they've remained friends, that shows you what a great guy you're marrying. Some guys discard women and never even think about remaining friends because they're of no use to them. So the mistake here would be in *becoming* the problem by lapsing into insecurity, worrying if he still has feelings for her, if she was prettier, and so on. A nervous mind can create all kinds of worry scenarios. So just brush it off and think of it another way: She's just a woman he knows, and maybe what he learned in their relationship made him a better boyfriend to you. This woman might be the reason he was ready for marriage when you were. Now, if this ex still flirts with him and behaves inappropriately, explain to your groom that her behavior makes you very uncomfortable, and you feel strongly about her not being invited to the wedding. It would be a big mistake for her to *be* invited, since her attention-grabbing antics and past disrespect for you have no place in your wedding day. Don't turn this into a loyalty tug of war. He's loyal to you. He's marrying you. He just might have some mutual friends who would take issue with her not being invited. Make sure you know the intricacies of his issue with this before you attempt to lay down a rule on him. Always be partners in your decisions, and let him know that her presence would take some of the joy out of your day, and if she caused any problems at the wedding, you would have a very hard time getting over it, because you did request that she be left off the list. Let your groom know that this is a serious issue for you, and that you'd really like him to honor your request here. And see the gift in this mistake you've just avoided: It got you really working together as a team and represented the kinds of give-and-take that make for successful marriages. Thanks, ex-girlfriend!

The mistake would be in *becoming* the problem by lapsing into insecurity, worrying that he still has feelings for his invited ex-girlfriend, if she was prettier, and so on. He's marrying you, so prevent any mistakes by reclaiming your self-confidence.

56. Not following office protocol ⊘⊘

It's important to maintain a certain protocol when it comes to coworkers and bosses on your wedding guest list. You can invite just the office friends with whom you socialize, and not the entire department. Your boss should be invited if he or she gave you time off to plan the wedding, and if you have a great relationship. It's becoming a more common practice to invite the boss even if you have only a professional relationship, as well. Where you make a mistake is in inviting too many coworkers as a way to get more gifts. I'm hearing this more and more—from the coworkers who are offended that brides and grooms are inviting them to showers and weddings when they barely know them. That's a too-obvious grab for gifts. You need to know about that perception even if it's not your intention. You thought that it was the right thing to do as a matter of etiquette, inviting all rather than some, but it comes off as greedy. So draw the natural line to include only the colleagues you'd normally socialize with outside the office, those with whom you're close, those who have enjoyed discussing your wedding planning with you and perhaps suggested the caterer you hired, and the others will understand if they don't make the list. It's part of office culture to have groups, and the many outsiders don't get invited to everything.

57. Inviting people thinking they won't be able to attend ⊘⊗⊘

This is a *big* one. Lots of brides and grooms out there have actually had to change their wedding locations—at a huge loss of money in lost deposits—because they invited everyone in the family, even those overseas, thinking, "they won't come, but they'll send a gift." Guess what? They *do* come. Weddings are tops on people's lists of what they'll travel for, and they love the happy circumstance under which to spend time with loved ones. When wedding invitations show up, they're more likely than ever to say they'll attend. So don't make this mistake of sending the courtesy invite, banking on getting regrets and presents. It's not likely to go that way, and you've then opened yourself up to a huge expense of almost twice the guest list you expected.

> **OUCH!**
> Couples say they've not only had to change the location, but also the style from formal sit-down to casual cocktail party or desserts-only because of their 300-person guest lists, due to guests unexpectedly accepting invitations from a distance, and the same goes for engagement parties and showers. Everything got much, much bigger when those courtesy invites hit the mailbox.

58. Putting too much focus on who you don't want there ⊘⊘

Brides, grooms, and their families lose a lot of peace of mind by focusing on the divorcing couples or the eccentric aunt, the bratty kid, or the drug addict cousin who has to be invited but is certain to cause a scene. Forget worrying, because you can cause yourself far more unhappiness thinking about it for a year than what actually happens on the wedding day. In a large crowd of your supporters, most troubled guests would have the self-control not to act up, but even if there is a commotion, the site has people who can remove them. So if you feel yourself thinking too often about those you *have* to invite, balance it out by thinking more about those you *get* to invite.

DO: Put it in writing! Journal every night about who you're excited to celebrate with, who you want to dance with, special toasts you want to share, and how much it means to you that your dearest friends are all traveling into town for your big day. When you train yourself to accentuate these people, the troublemakers lose all power over you.

DON'T: Add fuel to your fire by making the unwanted guests a topic of conversation with others, venting to your friends about how much you don't like your cousin's date, or your friend's date. That only pours more of your attention on the issue, and gets your supportive friend to hold a grudge as well. That doesn't help anything and could cause additional problems on the wedding day when that troubled guest overhears your friends talking about how she always makes a scene at weddings. Better to just keep it quiet, and the issue will stay small.

CHAPTER 8

YOUR BRIDAL PARTY

*Y*ou can make a *lot* of mistakes when you create a bridal party, and some of them have long-lasting consequences. You're asking your friends and relatives to devote big chunks of time and money to participate in a ritual for *you*, and when they have busy lives or low funds, it's a tremendous gift when they agree to participate. So watch out for the following top mistakes that other brides and grooms have made with their bridal parties, some of them unexpected and most of them unintentional, so that you all enjoy this time and the wedding while remaining a close and loving inner circle.

59. Stressing over who to include in your bridal party ◎◎◎

It can be *very* difficult to take a stand and say no to any outside pressure to include a friend or a cousin in the bridal party. But what happens when the pressure comes from inside, from your own guilt over what would be proper to do? This is once-in-a-lifetime, after all, and being named to the bridal party is pretty much being named to your own list of favorite people.

When you don't ask someone to be in the bridal party, it might seem like you're saying, "you're not one of my favorite people." So the question becomes: What's the bigger mistake? Adding people to your bridal party list because you feel you have to? Or *not* including people on your list because you don't want to have to? With the first, you get a big bridal party and a dull sense of it being less special because those choices are not entirely from your heart. With the second, the fallout is that people question your decision, the friend who expected to be included is hurt, and you fear that any controversy over your sister not being involved is going to overshadow your wedding day. The bottom line is that you can't ask everyone that you want *and* everyone else who wants to be in your lineup. Only you can draw the right line with this one. Brides who have massive complications with who to include in the bridal party from among many sisters, cousins, and friends are solving the problem by just having one or two bridesmaids—going with the less-is-more approach. Grooms are part of the equation, often preferring the smaller bridal party if they just have a brother or two, and too many friends to choose from. So talk it out, see who is a must and what your heart says is the right decision on this one.

IT'S NOT JUST ABOUT YOU

When you're asking people to be in your bridal party, keep in mind that you're asking them to devote a significant amount of time and money to your wedding. Dresses can cost $100, then shoes for $50, hair and makeup, then travel and a hotel room, showers, gifts . . . it can add up. So be very aware of the obligations that go into being in a bridal party before you ask anyone to participate.

60. **Asking his sisters to be bridesmaids when you don't know them very well** ◌◌

If you don't know his family very well but you want to make a good impression, you might consider asking his sisters to be bridesmaids. It's a lovely expression of inclusion. But what happens when his three sisters' inclusion means that your bridal party turns into a group of ten or some other number that strikes you as too big? It's always a gut feeling when it comes to building your bridal party, so this is a mistake *only* if you feel uncomfortable asking women you don't know to stand on your side. This is a decision you have to be comfortable with, because when you're dealing with people and the honor of being named to your bridal party, every one has to be special to you.

DO: Talk to your groom about the new trend of having his sisters stand on *his* side. We've gotten rid of the gender thing, and brides are having their brothers stand up for them, grooms having their sisters on their side. This could be the perfect solution.

DON'T: Feel like you have to include the groom's sisters and sisters-in-law, but do have a discussion with them about it. This is tricky, because it's not an easy conversation to have, but it's way better than just avoiding the issue and hiding from the topic. Simply say, "I've thought about this a lot, and [groom] and I would love it if you would stand in our bridal party. It would be even more special if you would be part of [groom's] lineup, since I'm having my brother stand on my side." This being a fairly new trend, you might have to explain that it's becoming more common, and that groomswomen get their choice—they can wear stylish black dresses *or* the dress the bridesmaids are wearing.

It's a mistake to ask them if you feel uncomfortable asking women you don't know, like his sisters or cousins, to stand on your side.

61. Asking those who didn't make the bridal party to hand out programs ◎◎

Find a great way to include friends or family who don't make the bridal party, but steer clear of asking them to hand out the programs or the bubble bottles—those tasks have become known as consolation prizes and aren't any kind of makeup gesture for being out of the bridal party.

DO: Ask these people to act as greeters, standing at the entrance to the church or the reception hall, welcoming guests warmly, offering to take digital photos of guests upon their arrival, directing guests to the coat check or to the champagne bar . . . these friends become the hospitality VIPs of your party in this arena.

DON'T: Apologize profusely, which becomes a problem in itself. Yes, it's disappointing for both of you that they can't be in the bridal party, but if you get too dramatic or overly apologetic, somehow it registers as your putting on an act, being disingenuous. Suddenly, this slighted friend is doubly insulted when you take your "I'm *so* sorry" routine too far. Just let it go and move on to another topic.

62. Feeling like you need even numbers ⊘

This is one of the most common questions that I receive through my website. No, you don't have to have even numbers of bridesmaids and groomsmen, so don't make the mistake of asking a few extra almost-friends to be bridesmaids just so you have someone to walk with the groom's friends. Now, it's become more common that an uneven bridal party means that a groomsman escorts two women back up the aisle during the recessional. No problem at all. If it's a case of you having two bridesmaids and the groom having six groomsmen, it can still work wonderfully in person and in the pictures. So don't obligate additional friends to be in the bridal party if it's not strongly in your wishes.

63. Not asking a friend to be in the bridal party just because she will be pregnant at the time ⊗⊗⊗

They make gorgeous maternity dresses now, and pregnant bridesmaids are glowing and beautiful. It's a big mistake to avoid asking a friend that you would have asked if she were not pregnant, because that amounts to judgment. That friend is going to be very hurt, and might feel that you don't want her involved because she's not going to be a size 2 on your wedding day. Ask your dear friend anyway, and let her make the decision as to whether or not she can commit to the responsibility, if she will be able to travel safely, and if she can make the financial commitment as well.

64. Not asking a friend to be in the bridal party because of how expensive it will be ⊗⊗⊗

This is where good-hearted concern goes too far. You know that your friend the starving artist would find it difficult to afford the designer dress and the travel, and especially a shower, so you plan to save her the financial stress by not asking her to be in the bridal party. There are very few insults larger than that one, especially if she ever finds out *why* you left her off the list. Never put a friendship in jeopardy over money. Ask her with only your wish for her to participate in mind, and not with "an out" in the form of "well, it's going to be *really* expensive, so I wouldn't be hurt if you don't want to do it." That's making a bad situation worse, not making you look like the most considerate friend ever. This might sound ridiculous, but there have been tons of wedding couples who have made this faux pas in a misguided attempt to do the right thing but still show that they're being thoughtful about a friend's life situation. Just ask, and let anyone who's in a tough spot—including students, those who live far away, new parents, those in law school or medical school—make the decision on their own. If they say no, *then* you show your thoughtful side by taking that no gracefully.

Never put a friendship in jeopardy over money.

65. Not letting them know what you expect ⊘⊘⊘

When someone agrees to be in your bridal party, they need to know what to expect. What's the wedding date, or if a date hasn't been set, is there a season that you have in mind? What's the location? Will it be in your hometown, or a destination wedding? And beyond the basics, which you need to inform them about as soon as you know for sure, there's the issue of how you'll expect them to plan with you. Is there going to be a celebratory dinner where you'll toast your bridal party and then give them the scoop on how the planning will progress? Is there going to be a bridesmaid's lunch when everyone is in town for Thanksgiving? Will you do everything via e-mail? If you can, send them a link to an article that describes the traditional bridal party members' roles that you'll abide by, and that gives them a monthly timetable that you're operating by as well. It won't do to have them all in the dark, not knowing when you expect them to deliver, and then having you call with a week's deadline to send their measurements or a dress deposit. You have to outline what you expect so that they can realistically arrange their schedules and their finances with plenty of time so that it doesn't pain them in any way. Not doing so says that you have them at your beck and call, and that they have to jump when you say so. That's no way to treat a friend.

DO: Ask each and every one of your bridal party members what their upcoming commitments are, such as moving, or final exams, a vacation already planned, so that you can work around their schedules. That's the best way to arrange how your group will operate, and it's the most gracious way for you to start off.

DON'T: Expect that they have to report in to you if they want to plan a vacation during the year of your engagement. Be flexible, and know that these adults in your bridal party have busy lives of their own, and they don't revolve around your wedding.

66. Choosing very young child attendants ◎

In an effort to be all-inclusive, you might consider having all of your nieces and nephews as flowergirls and ring-bearers, junior bridesmaids and junior groomsmen. It's a lovely look to have a bunch of child attendants. But if you expect a two year old to walk down the aisle as instructed, tossing rose petals as instructed . . . big mistake. Always assign roles according to each child's age and maturity level, since even an eight year old can act like a toddler. Talk to parents about the best way to define each child's role . . . the littlest ones can walk down the aisle but then be seated with their parents, rather than having them stand up in line with the bridal party. When you ask a too-young child to take wedding rituals seriously, that's just asking for trouble.

67. Assigning important roles to child attendants who would prefer not to have the spotlight ◎◎

Would it be great if your niece wore angel wings and danced down the aisle to the sounds of Mozart? Um, not if she's twelve. Some kids do *not* want the spotlight, and they may not know how to say no to you when you ask. They're taught to respect adults and be agreeable, so you might get a shy yes when you ask a child to do a reading or light a candle as part of the ceremony, but deep down inside that kid is screaming "don't make me do this!" This is a common occurrence when it's a second wedding and parents who are blending their families think it would be great to take vows with the kids, or have the kids do a reading for their new stepparent, or somehow join together with the new stepsiblings as a way to encourage bonding and show what a happy family you all are. That can be a ticket to disaster. So ask child participants what they would *like* to do as part of the wedding, if anything at all, and adjust your own expectations. It would be a mistake to put so much responsibility on a small child, or even on a teenager, both of whom know what they're comfortable with and what they'd rather not do.

> **Don't try to force kids to perform roles they're not comfortable with. Ask them what they'd like to do, and allow them to scale back their responsibility level so they too can enjoy the day.**

68. Indulging group antics ◎◎◎

Sigh ... why do some groups turn into packs of animals, ganging up on one person or excluding another? Why does the gossip have to start, judgments made over a bridesmaid whose suggestions are not trendy, whose shoes are not stylish? If you've mashed together disparate friends and relatives, immature ones at that, and group dynamics are veering into the "mean girls" category, put a stop to it now. You won't entertain any rude comments about your friends, and while you can't make them all become close, you will demand that they treat each other with respect. It's a *huge* mistake for a bride or groom, whether out of surprise or shyness or wanting to fit in with their own clique, to allow or participate in any teasing or gossip or other harshness toward anyone in the bridal party or toward other friends or guests. You're above it, so bring your group above it as well. This kind of game isn't going to take place anywhere near your wedding.

DO: Talk directly with the mean girls, or with the guys who are mercilessly teasing one of the other guys. Let them know that you don't appreciate the games, and if the games continue, there will be consequences.

DON'T: Tell the victim not to take it seriously. That friend didn't sign up for *this* kind of treatment. Let her know that you've got her back.

69. Becoming the boss ◎◎◎

No one likes a bully. So don't take this brief era of being in charge too seriously. Contrary to what they show on silly television shows, it's not cute when a bride makes her bridesmaids sign up for bootcamp to get in shape for the wedding day, and it's not acceptable to leave angry messages for a bridesmaid who wasn't home to take your call. Power may be intoxicating, but there's no excuse for bad behavior toward your bridal party. "You *said* you'd do anything I asked of you" is taking a friend's loving offer of "I'm here for you anytime" and twisting it into servitude. Even if you're joking around, don't make the mistake of acting like you're the boss.

Part Two

THE FUN BEGINS ...

*H*ere's where we get into the planning aspects of the wedding—your meetings with your vendors, the choices you're making (or not making) for the wedding-day details, and especially the intricacies of all the different industries like catering and floral design that you might not know enough about to avoid some of the worst and costliest mistakes. I'm saving you trial-and-error problems here by letting you in on the most common mistakes that other brides and grooms have made in all areas of their wedding so that *you* have the best chance at a problem-free wedding-planning experience and an as-near-to-perfect-as-possible dream wedding day.

CHAPTER 9

LOCATION ISSUES

The locations of your ceremony and reception are of great importance for their beauty and for their function. It's the latter that presents the greatest challenge when it comes to avoiding some of the most common wedding mistakes, so keep the following issues in mind when you're touring sites. If you've already booked your locations, it's not too late to avoid mistakes with them! Just call the site manager to ask about these topics, and put plans in motion to handle any issues now.

70. Choosing a place that needs a lot brought in ⊗⊗⊗

If you've booked a hotel ballroom or a plain party room at a restaurant, you may love the expanse of the room, the big picture windows, the shiny dance floor, but will you have access to extra tables for the disc jockey's setup, or for the dessert buffet? Ask about whatever you don't see in the room—don't assume that the site has long tables for you to use. It would be a bad surprise and an extra expense if you have to rent the tables or platforms you need. In the design category, what would your florist or wedding coordinator have to ship to your site? A big wrought-iron canopy as your ceremony backdrop? A chuppah that can be decorated your way? Does the site have a plain metal chuppah that you can use? For an outdoor wedding where you'll have a tent at the site, ask about the kitchen facilities at the establishment. Is it big enough for your caterer to use, or would your caterer need his or her own separate tent, bringing in ovens, warming tables, and refrigeration units? Are there restroom facilities at your site, or would you need to rent a portable restroom facility? Think about the function of the site as a key ingredient to your planning, so that you're not hit with big rental expenses.

WHAT THE SITE MIGHT HAVE

Some sites have outdoor bistro tables and wrought iron chairs, couches that can be set up outdoors, tables in different shapes, pedestals on which you can place floral décor, lights to hang from the trees, and other valuable items they invested in for other big events that are available for your use. Perhaps for free. It would be a huge mistake to pay for rentals of these types of items and then find out, while they're being delivered, that you could have had similar items for free.

71. Choosing a place that will charge a site fee ✏

The botanical gardens near you are *gorgeous*. So many beautiful trees and flowering plants will be in bloom, and there's an area that has waterfalls and fountains, a rock garden, and a koi pond. It's the perfect, dreamy location ... but it costs $5,000 to use for the day. Just to be on the grounds. Not including any of your existing wedding expenses like catering and flowers. Before you tour and fall in love with a beautiful garden or estate home, do some research online to see if that site charges a site fee. If you find that they charge a hefty amount that would be painful to add to the budget, do yourself a favor and don't even make an appointment to see the place. What good would it do to spend an afternoon touring a site you can't afford, one that will only set the bar too high and cause you to be disappointed in any other sites that are more realistic for your wedding plans?

DO: Call to ask if the site waives its booking fees during the off-season. If they're not busy during early spring, for instance, they may agree to drop that $5,000 fee just to get your business. It never hurts to ask. Check the websites for your state park system as well as your regional tourism office, plus garden clubs, for recommendations of gardens and beautiful settings that don't charge such high prices for use of their grounds. A wedding coordinator will know the best garden locations for less, so consider hiring a professional just for this task.

DON'T: Cut fifty people off of your guest list in order to afford the site fee. There are plenty of beautiful gardens to choose from, many of which charge lower site fees or perhaps none at all.

72. **Booking a site without seeing it in season** ⊘⊘⊘

If the timing works, call to ask for a tour of the grounds before you book it, in the season that your wedding will occur. So that would be the previous April if you've booked an April wedding. That's the only way to see what their landscapers have planted, if the tulips will be up and what color they will be. Would that sea of red tulips look strange with your green and pink color scheme? Are those trees going to be in bloom with cherry blossoms? It would be a mistake not to know the colors that will be around your site, since your designs could be ruined by a very pink, very Victorian garden look that makes your more modern floral pieces look out of place. And you could find that the site has such great landscaping, so many trees in bloom, that you won't need to spend thousands on a floral designer to provide any additional accent at all. It's the brides and grooms who don't look at the site—or photos of the site in bloom—that make the big mistake.

73. **Not reviewing the contract to see what's allowed and what's not** ✒ ⊘⊘⊘

It's all right there in the contract, but many brides and grooms miss it. And then they're stunned when the site manager says they don't allow tents to be staked into the ground, they don't allow parquet dance floors to be laid down on their lawn, they don't allow flash photography in the church, or some other rule that means you spent a *lot* of money for nothing . . . the items you arranged are not allowed, and that news comes down on the wedding day. While you're getting your hair done. *Big* mistake.

DO: Ask the site managers at both your ceremony and reception locations for detailed lists of what's not allowed on the grounds or in the building. They usually have a printout, since this is such an important question. That's where you find out that they don't allow guests to toss rose petals at you, or they don't allow sparklers, no candles on the tables due to fire hazards, and no alcohol out on the beach where you planned to have the cocktail party.

DON'T: Expect that "you didn't tell us" is going to work in getting them to allow you to bend their rules, or that they'll reimburse you for the things you purchased that you cannot use. The responsibility for reading the contract fully, and asking the key question of what's not allowed, is yours alone. You'd lose in court if there's a contract that spells out the limits.

Ask the site managers at both your ceremony and reception locations for detailed lists of what's not allowed on the grounds or in the building.

74. Not ensuring guest accessibility ⊘⊘⊘

Most sites have wheelchair-access ramps or elevators that guests can use, but when you choose an alternative site like a park or beach or a backyard, you'll need to think about whether or not guests in wheelchairs, those who use walkers, or those who have trouble with stairs can reach your wedding sites and move around them once they're there. A rocky path is going to be arduous for the elderly, as well as for guests who wear stiletto heels. That's a bad surprise to spring on them when they arrive for your wedding, something that guests will think "they should have told us about this!" So ask about separate access roads for those paths that lead to the beach. Is there a different way to get there? If some guests can walk through the wooded path to the lake or the reception site, can others be driven down a road? Many sites have gravel access roads for their utility trucks and landscapers' vehicles, so by asking this question, you avoid a big mistake of not ensuring your guests' comfort. You don't want any falls or turned ankles on the way to your ceremony or reception.

ASK WHAT THEY NEED

Add a line to your personalized wedding website, inviting guests to let you know about any accessibility problems they may have, since the path to the ceremony runs through a wooded area or is hilly. You'll be happy to make arrangements for easier travel and access, and you welcome their requests. It's never a mistake to prethink guests' needs and invite their input.

75. Choosing a site that's dangerous for children ⊘⊘⊘

As much as you'd like to think that parents will watch their children during the wedding, many parents just let their kids run free. If there are rocky paths and pools with no fences, ponds that the little ones can fall into while reaching for the pretty fish, you have an enormous danger zone on your hands, and the makings of a tragedy. So if children will be on your guest list, look at your potential sites through the eyes of a protective mom—or bring along your most protective-mom friend for her opinions. You might find that the site just poses too many risks for unattended children. *Don't* ask the site manager to post any signs about dangerous areas, thinking that will solve the problem. Kids tend to ignore signs and go where their curiosity takes them.

76. Choosing sites that are too far apart ⊘

This is more of an annoyance than anything else. When you select a ceremony site in one town, and then the reception site in a town that's more than an hour away, you put an extra burden on guests, especially when you don't allow enough time for traffic and other delays. You don't want your guests—or you—to travel under stress, so choose locations that are closer together, and provide good written directions.

DO: Test out the written directions that you find on Map-Quest and other driving directions sites. All too often, they include mistakes—this would be disastrous! Use the directions cards from your reception site not just in your invitations but written out on your personalized wedding website or e-mailed to guests the week before the wedding.

DON'T: Expect that guests will automatically use MapQuest and other driving directions sites when you give them a street address. Not everyone uses high-tech gadgets like GPS systems, so you're going to get a *ton* of phone calls and e-mails asking for directions.

77. Choosing a site with no weather protection plan ⊘⊘⊘

You love the outdoor setting for your dream garden wedding, but the site has no indoor ballroom or other space for guests to get out of the elements. The mistake is in putting yourselves at the mercy of the weather. A tent may shield you from rain, but what happens if it's an unseasonably cold or hot day outside? When you're planning an outdoor wedding, always make sure you choose a location that offers both indoor and outdoor space where guests can go for their own comfort. Great establishments will assure you that they can set up your ceremony chairs and décor outside where you originally planned, but they have the staff and the method to move everything inside to the ballroom with just forty-five minutes' notice. *That's* the place you want to be.

> **The mistake is in putting yourselves at the mercy of the weather.**

78. Choosing a site that hosts more than one wedding at a time ⊘⊘⊘

You don't want to be just one of the weddings going on that day. You don't want to hear the other wedding's music through the walls, or hear the other wedding's rowdy guests walking by your ballroom doors during your first dance. And you definitely don't want the site's B-team servers working your wedding while their elite staff is working the other wedding. You don't want strain on the site's power capabilities, or strangers walking into your wedding reception because the food is better. So choose a site that hosts only one wedding on the grounds at a time, and you'll get 100 percent of their top-notch service as well as an avoidance of distraction.

79. Choosing a site that requires you to use their experts ⊘⊘⊘

Some banquet halls or unique settings like museums or estate homes require that you use their own staff. That means you have to use their caterer, their florist, their photographer—the vendors that the site manager knows and has a business partnership with. Not getting to choose your own experts means that you might not get the absolute best florist in town, or the absolute best caterer. You'd be stuck with experts assigned to you, and their menus or packages might not be as varied as you might find elsewhere.

DO: Ask the site manager if you can have an exemption from their rule about using their experts. Some sites do allow a switch, and they'll adjust your price package accordingly.

DON'T: Attempt to just bring in your own experts on the day, thinking it would be easier to apologize than to ask permission. That might work in business, but it won't work at your wedding. Especially if the experts you hire are not aware that you're defying a site rule, they won't appreciate it when they're escorted out of the building for trespassing. And you lose all that money.

80. Choosing a site that has no place for photos ⊗⊗⊗

Uh oh. You were so taken with the site's prices and the pretty ballroom that you didn't even think about where you would go to take photos on the grounds. That means you'd all have to pile into cars and go to a gazebo, or get a permit from a local park for your photos to be taken there. Don't leave yourself without options for several different beautiful photo locations. Choose a site that offers great scenery, a marble terrace, a willow tree, a grand fireplace, or other areas that would be ideal for pictures.

DO: Ask the site manager where other couples have taken photos. You might find out that they have a private garden in the back that they open up for portraits, or a private room in the building where photos have been taken.

DON'T: Try to just take photos in the reception room. With all of the guests looking on, it's a huge distraction that entices bridal party members or parents to look away from the camera because they see something going on in the room. Always arrange for a private area for photos.

CHAPTER 10

CEREMONY DETAILS

The ceremony is the most important part of your wedding day, so extra care should be taken to prevent anything that could go wrong. You might hear very often that you can't control everything that happens on your wedding day, but many of these details are things you *can* control. And quite easily, too.

81. Waiting too long to book your house of worship ⊗⊗⊗

You might think you have all the time in the world to book your ceremony site, but it's actually one of the first things you need to do. Some churches and synagogues are booked two years in advance, with weddings in the morning, afternoon, and evening! Especially if you live in a town where there are few houses of worship, you have lots of competition in the form of all the other wedding couples out there trying to get their time slot. Add in the confusion of some houses of worship having rules about not booking weddings on a Saturday morning (for a noon reception) because they have a rule of keeping mornings open for funerals, and you could wind up in a very frustrating situation. I'm hearing from more couples that the scheduling process for booking house of worship weddings was so complicated that they decided not to marry in a house of worship at all. There was just too much conflict about available dates and times, and they didn't want to move their reception into a more expensive time slot for an evening celebration. So get on this now, and ask about the site's additional rules, such as required premarital classes, any fees or additional staff that has to be hired (some require you to pay their site maintenance person who would open the church and oversee the event), and their house rules such as no flash photography. All of the myriad details add up, making the booking of a house of worship a more labor-intensive process than you might expect. Not knowing about this would be a big mistake and a tough way to start your wedding plans. So be prepared to make a lot of calls, take a lot of meetings, and ask a lot of questions.

DON'T TAKE ON THE CHURCH

Don't think that you can show up at the house of worship and do all the things they said you can't—like have flash photography or bare your shoulders—and no one is going to say anything. Even if they don't remove you, which they might, it's still quite rude to disrespect the house rules, and yes, they may say something about it in front of your guests.

82. **Not knowing the rules about your marriage license** ◎◎◎

It's your wedding day, your ceremony was beautiful, but your marriage license has expired. So in the eyes of the law, you're not really married. You're going to have to apply for another license and have a separate ceremony to make it official. Or, you applied for your marriage license the day before the wedding, only to find out that there's a three-day waiting period for the license to be valid. You have to know the current rules about your "piece of paper" so that your marriage is legal and valid in the state.

DO: Call the county registrar and find out your state's and town's rules about marriage licenses. Each jurisdiction has its own rules, many with different waiting periods and requirements for application. So talk to a person about what you need to bring, when you need to go, and the window of viability for your license. Be very detail-oriented with this step, since it would be a colossal mistake for your license to be expired or not in your hands at all on the wedding day.

DON'T: Depend on what you read on websites, since many regional bridal websites have outdated articles on their sites, and some inaccuracies may be up there as well. Or, a law just changed, and it hasn't made it onto the government website yet. Always deal with a live person, *in* person if possible.

83. **Not knowing a house of worship's rules about membership** ⊘⊘

It's the church that you've attended for years, the church where your parents got married, and where you attended childhood schools and camps. That would qualify you as a member, right? Not necessarily. This is one of the most frustrating things that brides and grooms run into when they're trying to plan their ceremonies—a house of worship might have strict rules that they will only perform marriage rites for members of their congregation. And by members, that means you're signed up on their list, you contribute money, you volunteer, and so on. Sometimes it's an official at the church or synagogue who has one of those difficult personalities, who wants to rule his or her congregation with an unexpected iron fist. And you are *not* members if you don't meet their criteria. This is sad, but true in some cases around the country. So make sure you ask about membership requirements, and what the house of worship's policy is on performing wedding ceremonies for those who don't belong but would like to honor their family's wishes for a church wedding.

DO: Find out if they'd accept your joining their list now and making a financial contribution for membership, if you really want to get married there.

DON'T: Book your wedding date with an office clerk, thinking you can meet with the officiant when the wedding date gets closer. It would be a horrific mistake to find out a month before the wedding that they've just discovered you're not a member. Be sure to cover all the bases and meet early with the officiant who will perform your ceremony.

84. Not honoring the rules about who can marry you ⊘⊗⊘

Check with your town's marriage registrar for the list of who is recognized as an *official* wedding officiant allowed to perform legal and valid marriage ceremonies. You'll receive a list that might include the following: the mayor, judges of the superior and appellate court, town council members, and officiants from any *recognized* religion. That word can throw a challenge at you. What exactly counts as a *recognized* religion? Be sure to ask. In our age of Internet ordainment, anyone can pay $25 to get a certificate saying they're an ordained minister from the Church of the Cheeseburger, and they expect that qualifies them to perform a marriage ceremony. Nope. Family members and friends can be ordained for the day only in certain states—California being one of them at the time of this writing—so make sure you research the going rules well before you promise your uncle that he can preside over your wedding rites. That town marriage registrar will know the Internet ordainment sites that are officially sanctioned by the state, and he or she can check with the state's higher-ups for approval of any religious order that you belong to. We do have freedom of religion in this country, but when it comes to the law, they need to specify which officiants are valid. So work through these steps and get official, written approval for any officiant you'd like at your ceremony, or stick with the list of approved sources like the mayor or a judge. It would be awful to find out later that your independent minister was not actually licensed, and his signature on your marriage license is void. You're not really married.

IS RETIRED OKAY?

Check with your county's marriage license registrar to find out the rules of retired judges or former mayors as possible officiants. Some counties have varying rules on this, and you don't want to find out that your license is invalid because it's been signed by a retired judge. Yes, it says "judges" on the county list of officiants, but it's better to ask about this significant detail.

---

85. Not asking for changes to the script ◐◐

When you sit down with your officiant, it's easy to get a little bit intimidated and just listen to them tell you how the ceremony is going to be. They're experienced. They're an authority figure. They know what they're doing. And some officiants like to stick to their own scripts because they're comfortable with them. But it would be a mistake *not* to go through that script line-by-line and change some wording, add in personal statements, delete some things you're not comfortable with. This is your ceremony, the centerpiece of your day, and every word has to resonate with you. You have to make sure that every reading is one that you're happy with, every poem meaningful, every part of your vows or the candle ceremony fitting exactly what you dreamed of for your wedding. Most officiants want to help you do this, and they may give you a questionnaire. Take this seriously, and plan several planning sessions as bride and groom so that you can record what you do want said and what you don't want said. Speak up about the tone you want: a formal, solemn ceremony, or a laid-back ceremony with lots of humor and light moments. The officiant wants to please you as well, so work together to get the wording just right.

DO: Ask to take their script home so you can work on it. Don't be pressured to work on it right there and get it done *now*.

DON'T: Stick with an officiant who won't let you change the script, or who tries to insert his or her own spiritual readings because "that's the way I do it." You need to weed out the officiants who just want to perform so that your ceremony is led by someone who can put the focus on you.

86. Not explaining rituals ⊘

Your guests need to know what's going on during your ceremony so that they can fully appreciate the beauty and symbolism of all of your religious and cultural rituals. Otherwise, there will be a palpable sense of confusion in the crowd as they all look at one another shrugging and whispering, "why is the mother throwing figs at them?" (That's a cultural ritual symbolizing abundance in some cultures.) Use your wedding program as the perfect place to explain each ritual, which further involves your guests and enlightens them about the wonderful rites in your culture. And if part of your ceremony will take place in a different language, provide the translation in print as well. It would be a mistake to leave guests out of the loop.

87. Having jokes or surprises in a solemn ceremony ◎◎

It starts off as a good idea, something that the groom thinks will create a fun, light mood during a solemn ceremony and be more "him" than what he knows is planned. But no one appreciates that he's written a message on the soles of his shoes, saying "Help me!" that everyone can see when he's kneeling during the ceremony. When groomsmen take it upon themselves to hold up scorecards rating that first kiss ("10!" "9.5!" "I've seen better!"), a few guests might laugh, but the parents are going to be steamed. So don't allow any surprises during the ceremony. Tell the groom to keep his sense of humor to the rehearsal dinner, and tell those groomsmen that their usual pranks are not to be part of the ceremony itself. When you speak up now, you get some peace of mind. This is not to say that no surprises can be planned, of course. The groom may want to surprise his bride with the performance of a song he wrote for her. That's sweet and adds to the romance of the day. But when you have a guest who dresses up like Spiderman and runs through the room as comic relief, it ruins the entire effect of the ceremony. Again, this isn't a show, it's your wedding. So if you know that some of your bridal party members are pranksters, lay down the law that they are to leave your ceremony alone.

> This isn't a show, it's your wedding. So tell pranksters to keep their jokes to the rehearsal dinner and leave your big day alone.

88. Getting a cheap aisle runner ⊘

Don't get talked into a cheap aisle runner as a way to save money and still have that traditional item, since many of those inexpensive aisle runners are actually more like giant rolls of paper towels that many couples and guests trip over. Beyond the fact that these cheap aisle runners don't adhere to the ground, your heels can get caught in the fabric, causing you to stumble on your way down the aisle.

DO: If you want an aisle runner, invest in a good one with traction edges (a strip of rubber along both sides to grip the floor), a pretty material, and any design flourishes. Or skip the aisle runner—as is a modern trend—to allow for better color contrast between your gown and a dark floor. It's such a lovely look!

DON'T: Choose an aisle runner that has tassels on the edges, since guests have been known to trip on those as well.

89. Not arranging for temperature control ◇◇◇

Especially when your ceremony will be lengthy, such as with a mass, make sure you ask the site manager to turn on the air conditioner or heat in the ceremony site at least an hour before guests arrive. You don't want it to be sweltering in there, because that turns into a fainting hazard (not to mention it makes for cranky children). It should be comfortable in the room, and you do have the power to make sure that is so.

90. Not checking if your site is open for a rehearsal the night before the wedding ◇◇◇

This applies to a house of worship ceremony setting or *any* setting such as having your ceremony in the garden at the reception site. You *have* to book it for your rehearsal as soon as humanly possible. Again, there's a lot of competition for house of worship time slots on the weekends, so there may be two or three weddings slated for that Saturday. So that means multiple groups vying for the Friday night rehearsal. At a non-church location, you may not get access to the grounds for a rehearsal due to a wedding taking place there the night before. So make your plans early, and if your site isn't available, know that you can enact your rehearsal at *any* location such as your home where your rehearsal dinner will be. Just line up your bridal party, tell them how to walk, let them know what to expect during the ceremony, and instruct on the recessional and any possible receiving line. Then let the rehearsal dinner begin!

DON'T WING IT

Brides and grooms whose locations are not available for rehearsals sometimes see that as an opportunity to skip the rehearsal altogether. "We'll just tell everyone their positions on the wedding day," they say. But those first bridesmaids will need to know exactly where to walk to, child attendants should never be thrown into an unpracticed processional, and the recessional definitely needs to be practiced, especially if you have an uneven number of bridesmaids and groomsmen. It's a big mistake not to do at least one run-through, or to take the word of the site staff that they'll instruct everyone on the wedding day.

CHAPTER 11

FOOD AND DRINK

*W*hat's on the menu for your wedding? The feast might include an extravagant cocktail party spread with amazing stations and passed hors d'oeuvres, a five-course sit-down dinner, a gorgeous cake, and plenty of champagne to go around. Knowing that the reception is the majority of a wedding budget, you may have worked some magic in creating unique dishes with the caterer, and found some wonderful ways to provide fabulous food for less money. Your goal is to feed your guests well, give them delicious dishes they don't get at every wedding, and have everyone raving about the food and cake for long after the wedding. If you make some of the most common mistakes in this category, though, guests tend to consider the *entire* wedding a flop. Such is the importance of the catering aspect for your wedding, and again, there are some major mistakes you can prevent—like food poisoning— by being aware of the most common missteps.

91. Not enough food for not enough time ⊗⊗⊗

In a misguided effort to save money on the most expensive part of the wedding (again, food often adds up to 60 percent of a wedding budget), some brides and grooms figure they can cut corners by serving fewer items at the cocktail party, and serving food for a shorter amount of time. Taken to the extreme, that leaves guests hungry and quite angry at you for not caring enough to feed them a satisfying meal after they've traveled so far to attend your wedding, and perhaps given you a generous gift. "Cheaping out" on the food impresses no one and is the number-one mistake when it comes to your catering.

DO: Provide lots of different food choices, and work with your caterer to select items that are on the lower-end of the cost scale. Talk about in-season seafoods and meats, and use seafood as a garnish rather than having a seafood bar or other pricy offering. Your caterer or chef has tons of ideas for stretching a food budget; they've mastered the art of creativity with the less expensive items like chicken, pasta, and vegetarian dishes, even meats and seafoods, so there's no reason for you to limit the food choices when so much can be prepared well.

DON'T: Allow a block of time during your wedding where no food is being served at all. The dancing hours shouldn't be starvation time. So stagger the presentation of food stations if you have to, but do have enough food for it to be a bounty.

"Cheaping out" on the food impresses no one and is the number-one mistake when it comes to your catering.

92. Offering super-cheap food and drinks to save money ⊘⊘⊘

Guests can tell when you've cheaped out by serving just pasta and finger sandwiches. They've been to enough weddings and planned enough special events of their own to know what things cost in the catering world. So even if you are on a budget, don't select *all* super-cheap foods. Mix in a few pricier options along with that pasta bar. And never choose the cheapest wines and liquors possible. Go mid-shelf rather than top-shelf to save money, but don't sacrifice taste for dollars. Guests have sophisticated tastes and they don't want to drink inferior wines at your wedding. You don't want to leave them with (literally) a bad taste in their mouths. So ask for a wine tasting, or get the names of their house wines, buy a bottle at a discount liquor store, and have a tasting on your own to make sure you know these vintages taste wonderful.

93. Having a cash bar ⊘⊘⊘

It's *never* okay to have a cash bar at a wedding, and you shouldn't even allow a tip jar to be out on the bartop. These are your wedding guests, so they should never have to open their wallets at your event. If you need to save money, limit your bar options to wine and beer only, plus one or two mixed drinks like martinis or Jack and Coke if you must, and specify that no shots are to be served to any guests. That's simply not on your bar menu. Some couples have tried to beat the bar tab by placing one or two bottles of wine on each guest table, but those get emptied within the first half-hour of the wedding. Guests have been so angry about the placement of two wine bottles that they have gone out and purchased their own bottles of wine at a nearby liquor store, for their table only, and then other guests complain, not knowing that the contraband is a personal stash. I've read on a wedding message board that some brides and grooms are giving out drink tickets to their guests, as in "this ticket good for one drink at the bar." What the heck is that? This is a wedding, not a carnival! Never give out tickets for guests' drinks, or you'll look incredibly rude, tacky, and cheap.

DO: Close the bar early, such as an hour before the reception ends, as a way to save money.

DON'T: Allow guests to bring in their own liquor. Most sites don't allow outside supply, and you don't want a scene when the site manager confiscates bottles or stops someone from walking in the door with cases of beer.

It's *never* okay to have a cash bar at a wedding, and you shouldn't even allow a tip jar to be out on the bartop.

94. Trying to do too much on your own or with volunteers ⊘⊘⊘

Again, as a way to save money, you might think that you can prepare all of the food, and the cake, yourself. Or have volunteers do all the cooking for the wedding. I'd suggest that you steer clear of the kitchen that weekend. Don't pile up your obligations, because there is a *lot* that will have to be done at the last minute. If you have volunteers cooking for any wedding event, such as the rehearsal dinner, make sure you're only accepting their offers to help, not assigning dishes for them to bring. You don't want to turn your wedding into a potluck, or obligate people to find a way to not only cook the food, but transport it in a way that keeps it refrigerated, and then find a way to reheat it and plate it for service. That's a lot of work. For self-cooked food, keep that to the rehearsal dinner, engagement party, and showers for the most realistic use. If guests will bring food to the reception, ask them to bring platters that don't need such strict refrigeration or heating rules, such as platters of cut fruit or trays of brownies as an accent to your dessert bar. Make it easy for them to contribute.

95. **Leaving food out in hot weather** ⊘⊘⊘

When you work without a trained caterer, you run the risk of food dangers. Foods and sauces that are left out in hot weather can go bad, and anyone who eats them could get a bad case of food poisoning, which is a top mistake in self-catered weddings. Cheeses and mayonnaise-based dishes are especially vulnerable to the heat, as is seafood. Salads wilt, and some wedding cakes have been known to soften and slide to the ground! So don't make the mistake of leaving food outside, even in the shade. Have all foods served indoors where it's cooler, and plan to have that wedding cake brought out from a refrigerator just before it's cut and served.

DO: Talk to your caterer about the plan for keeping foods cold in hot weather. You'll learn about ice trays and how the servers will bring trays back inside to switch them up with cold platters. A professional knows the rules about food and heat, so this is another reason why it's worth it to invest in an expert for an outdoor wedding and leave the do-it-yourself approach to your smaller, at-home parties where everything is kept inside, also prepped for serving on ice platters.

DON'T: Think that shade and a fan will take care of the problem. When it gets hot outside, it doesn't take long for bacteria to build in certain foods.

RESEARCH FOOD SPOILAGE RULES

Visit *www.hgtv.com* for articles and advice on the length of time that meats, cheeses, creamy sauces, and icings can be left out without refrigeration.

96. Not having enough servers or bartenders ⊘⊘⊘

When your celebration is at home—whether it's the wedding itself or a prewedding party—make sure you don't skimp on the number of servers or bartenders you'll have. You don't want guests standing around waiting for food while the two servers you hired are running around, sweating, not getting three steps into the crowd before their platters are picked clean, and you don't want a five person-deep line at your bar. So spend the extra money for enough help, and you'll prevent one of the most common and most regrettable mistakes you can make at a wedding.

DO: Talk to your site manager or wedding coordinator about how many servers they will provide, and if the number seems low for your guest headcount, ask them to bring in more workers. They will usually be happy to meet your needs. But if they say, "That will be $50 more per server," agree to it. It's a great investment to have enough attentive help, rather than risk the big mistake of having too few wait staff.

DON'T: Forget to ask about this! It's a very important detail, one that many brides and grooms don't think about. They just assume that the site will provide enough help. And if you're planning your wedding at home or at a site that doesn't have a staff, it's not enough to just set up a buffet and expect everything to run smoothly. Find a staffing service online, or through your other wedding vendors, and hire your own experienced wait staff to assist with serving, clearing plates throughout the event (*very* important!), and cleaning up broken glasses.

97. Not asking about brand names for drinks ⊘⊘

Wedding coordinators have written to me in droves about this new mistake occurring more and more: don't forget to ask about the *brand* of soft drinks that will be served at the wedding. Many catering establishments are saving money by not having brand-name sodas like Coke or Pepsi or Sprite, but are instead loading their bars with no-name brands . . . and guests can tell. So this is a question you need to ask of the site or bar manager. Having off-tasting soft drinks can be just as bad as having off-tasting wines.

CHAPTER 12

ENTERTAINMENT

*T*he entertainment can make or break your wedding reception. A fantastic band with a great sound can keep the dance floor filled all night, with all of your favorite songs playing one after the other, the musicians performing elaborate numbers with pitch-perfect sound, and the lead singer getting everyone energized and involved in the show. A great disc jockey loads the perfect combination of songs, and the sound system is crystal-clear. And everyone says your wedding was the party of the century.

If you make mistakes, though, you could wind up with a cheesy band or a disc jockey in a sequined jacket dancing on top of a 1980s-era speaker, an empty dance floor, and so many breaks in the action that your party never gets off the ground. The decisions you make now can prevent these catastrophes, so keep the following mistakes in mind as you arrange the entertainment for your big day.

98. **Hiring a band or disc jockey after only seeing a DVD performance** ⊘⊘⊘

If you try to save time by asking a bunch of bands for their audition DVDs and then hiring on the basis of what you see in their taped performances, you're more likely to get bait-and-switched. Which means you'll wind up with a completely different band than the one you saw onscreen. Sure, the band has the same name, but the DVD was created a few years ago, and now there are all different band members in the group, a different lead singer, and an entirely different repertoire than you heard on that DVD. Instead of top hits, they play more 1980s music now, or—even worse—their new lead singer thinks he's Steve Perry from Journey, and that's all he can sing. You didn't hire a cover band, so who are these people performing the painful rendition of *Don't Stop Believing?* And why is he dressed like that? Brides and grooms across the country say this is their number-one regret when it comes to arranging for their entertainment. They will tell you, as I do, that you should invest the time to hold auditions or arrange to see each band or musical performer in action at a live event. That's the only way to get a good feel for their performance level, hear the quality of their instrumentals and sound system, see how the crowd responds to them, how they lead the party. And the same is true for musical performers at your ceremony or cocktail hour, those pianists and guitarists whose performances are important as well.

DO: Ask them or check their websites to find out where they are going to be performing, such as at a club in town, or at another wedding nearby this weekend. You *can* stop by an actual wedding and stand just outside the ballroom doors, maybe peek inside but don't go inside, to observe the band in action. For entertainers who aren't performing at any place you can get to, ask them when and where you can get together with them for a brief audition. You're not putting them out; they're used to auditioning, and they'll welcome the chance to show you their stuff. The live show is vitally important to catch any way you can.

DON'T: Let them tell you to just watch the video stream on their website. Videos can be edited, and again, you may not get the current incarnation of the band. If an entertainer won't give you a live show, or invite you to one, move on to the next contender on your list.

99. Not asking about the entertainer's break plans ⊘⊘⊘

This is something you need to have written into your contract with the entertainer. You're paying for a certain amount of performance time, and when a band plays for a half hour, then takes a fifteen minute break, plays for a half hour, takes a fifteen minute break, and so on, pretty soon you've lost an hour out of what you paid for, and the reception suffers from stop-and-go syndrome. So the mistake here is in forgetting to ask about breaks. Find out how many they take, and when they take them—such as, "when the cake is served, we play the cake-cutting music, and then we take a ten-minute break." You'll also need to ask them what happens during their breaks. Do they turn on MP3s of popular music, recordings of their own songs that they haven't yet played at the reception, piano instrumentals? What is it that your guests will be listening to? And can you have some say in the playlist for the break music? Or will the site need to pipe in music while they're away from their instruments? If they say they take four ten-minute breaks, then you'll need to talk about adjusting the payment since it's not truly a four-hour package. Having a mini-confrontation now is way better than being surprised on the wedding day or having your parents get upset that the band they hired isn't playing enough. It's the little, unexpected details like the amount and timing of breaks that trip up brides and grooms who *don't* have the inside scoop like you do.

You're paying for a certain amount of performance time, and when a band plays for a half hour, then takes a fifteen minute break, plays for a half hour, takes a fifteen minute break, and so on, pretty soon you've lost an hour out of what you paid for, and the reception suffers from stop-and-go syndrome.

100. **Not providing a playlist or a don't-play list** ⊘⊘⊘

You might think this would be a no-brainer, but there are couples out there who request a first dance song and the mother-son and father-daughter songs, and then say, "just play music that's good for the dinner hour," and "play all popular hits for the reception." Well, the entertainer might have a completely different idea of what's good for the dinner hour than you would expect, so you could wind up with music that's all classical, or ballads that come off as cheesy to your guests. Never leave the playlist to chance. Entertainers *want* you to micromanage and provide a detailed list of fifty songs to play during the reception. The entertainer *wants* to make sure that your dance floor is packed and that everyone has a great time. You know your guest list best, so it's up to you to say, "We'd like all slow dances during the dinner hour since most of our guests are in their thirties and forties and coupled-up; they'd rather dance to Michael Bublé and Tony Bennett than to Top 40 stuff during dinner."

DO: Ask the entertainer if he or she has a repertoire list of the songs that are possible, and also their Top 100 list of most popular wedding reception songs. You can also find these online at various disc jockey sites. Sit down with your groom and work through the list, crossing off songs you don't want and starring songs that are must-play. You'll then deliver this list to the band or disc jockey a few weeks before the reception (it would be a mistake to deliver it any closer to the wedding, since they have to prepare!), and your playlist is set.

DON'T: Leave it to chance, or forget to say "no line dances!" or "nothing that would be played in a baseball stadium!" or "absolutely *no* chicken dance!" These cheesy dances and songs can stop the momentum of a great wedding. Some of the most common no-play requests include the *Chicken Dance*, *Macarena*, country line dances, and conga lines.

Don't forget to nix any songs that remind you of a previous wedding or relationship, like the first dance song from your first marriage, or that of a recently divorced sibling.

101. **Not protecting song requests** ⊘⊗⊘

Tell your disc jockey that no one is to request a song and have it played without your okay. I know, it sounds a little bit controlling, but you really do need to have a rule in place, or you'll lose your own playlist in favor of some strange choices made by guests. It's a mistake to allow your disc jockey to play songs that remind you of your exes or your prior marriage, or to change the tone of your reception from slow-dancing classics to club dancing songs too early in the night, or have eyebrow-raising songs like "The Lady Is a Tramp" played while you and your bridesmaids are on the dance floor. And that cousin who eloped might try to get her first dance moment courtesy of your wedding! So make sure that your entertainer knows that requests have to be cleared through you, and that if you're not around, the answer is "no for now."

102. Not giving the phonetic pronunciation of your bridal party members' and parents' names—as well as your names ⊘⊘

The moment when you're all introduced into the room—first the parents, then the bridal party, and then the bride and groom—is one of the best moments of the reception. It's captured on video forever. So you *have* to make sure that the emcee or band leader pronounces everyone's names correctly! Tara might like her name pronounced TAH-ra instead of TARE-a, and your parents would have scowls on their faces during their entrance if their names are butchered. And getting *your* names wrong? That flattens the moment. So be sure to prewrite everyone's names out phonetically, as in the following model:

Best Man: John Smith
Maid of Honor: (TAH-ra) Ellison
Flowergirls: (JAY-na) and Jennifer Sloane

How upset would little Jana be if she were to be introduced as Janna? Kids have had meltdowns over less, so don't make the mistake of leaving name pronunciation up to a band leader, disc jockey, or emcee who doesn't know any of you. Entertainers *love* getting phonetic listings . . . it makes their jobs easier, and they get to make you happy.

CHAPTER 13

PHOTOGRAPHY AND VIDEOGRAPHY

The photos and videos from your wedding day are among the only tangible items that you will keep *forever*. They get even more valuable over time, when you can look back years later and see the smiling face of a grandparent who's no longer with you, or watch video of yourself dancing with your father when you were both younger. So consider this a very important category where you don't want to make these mistakes of inexperience, which are some of the most common, yet heartbreaking, down the road.

103. Leaving hiring until later ⊘⊘⊘

When you're just starting out with your wedding plans, make sure that securing your photographer and videographer are among the first vendor bookings you make. You want to make sure you have access to the best in the business, at fair prices. Due to the importance of their products, these are going to be expensive packages. So if you get right on the task, you'll avoid last-minute bookings at higher prices, and especially being left with only the most inexperienced experts in town since all the other area brides and grooms have snapped up the best pros.

DO: Ask your recently married friends for referrals to the photographers and videographers they loved, and also get referrals through your wedding coordinator and other wedding experts. You want first-hand accounts of how great a job they do, rather than choosing a pro because he has the biggest ad in the Yellow Pages.

DON'T: Hire the first experts you meet, just to get the job done. Always interview several, and you may find that you like that first one even more after a few ho-hum interviews.

104. Not submitting a photo wish list ◌◌

In the hectic rush between the ceremony and the reception, your group will have photos taken at a quick pace, so that you can all get to the cocktail party in time to enjoy it. Most photographers try to get all the bridal party, couple, and family photos taken in less than twenty minutes, so they depend on your written list of which portraits you want. The wisest couples write a checklist ahead of time of the must-have shots: the bride with her parents, the bride and groom with both sets of parents, the bride with the child attendants, and so on. What's the number-one picture most often forgotten? The bride, or the groom, with siblings. For some reason, no one thinks of that one! So don't even think about having a photo session without a printed list, or you'll miss a once-in-a-lifetime opportunity to get a cherished photo.

DO: Print out photo wishlists that you find online at wedding websites, and star the photos you want your photographer to capture. Assign a volunteer to read down the list, announcing which photo is up and which are upcoming, such as "groom's siblings, gather 'round. You're next." This way, each group can fluff their hair and straighten their ties before they're called before the lens.

DON'T: Get overly controlling with the list. If parents ask for an additional photo, it takes less time to just have the photographer snap it than it would to argue about it not being on the list.

Don't even think about having a photo session without a printed list, or you'll miss a once-in-a-lifetime opportunity to get a cherished photo.

105. Not getting copies for others ⊘⊘⊘

Prints of wedding photos can be expensive. Some photographers charge more than $20 for 4" × 6" prints, which can only be ordered through his website for copyright reasons. As the bride and groom, you might have budget issues, but this isn't the place to try to save some money. You should never require your parents, grandparents, or bridal party members to buy prints from your wedding day, so don't send them the link and expect them to buy online. These should be a gift from you, as a matter of good etiquette. They can, if they wish, buy enlargements or additional prints on their own, but you're better off getting a parents' album as well as a framed print for each bridal party member.

PHOTOGRAPH LIST

Make a list of the people for whom you'd like to buy photos, so that you don't forget anyone important, and ask your in-laws for their list of important relatives as well.

_____

_____

_____

_____

_____

_____

_____

_____

_____

_____

_____

_____

106. Not checking prices for prints others will order ✗

With most photographers offering digital images on their own websites, or through photo-sharing sites like Pictage, it's very important that you ask about the price per print as part of your interview process while considering which photographer to hire. Since everyone will be considering photos through his or her site, you need to know if this expert charges through the roof, or if his or her prices are in the moderate range.

DO: Let guests know the price per print in your e-mail to them, sharing the URL for the photos they may order. On some sites, guests are asked to register and provide their e-mail addresses, which many have strong feelings about. They don't want to get on a mailing list, or receive solicitations from your photographer. When you write, "Prints are $12.50 for a 5" × 7" and $15 for an 8" × 10", they may decide not to sign into the site at all. It's a very considerate action for you to provide this information in your greeting.

DON'T: Be afraid to ask the photographer for a print price list before you hire him or her. It's the sign of an informed consumer, and photographers expect this question up-front. They make their money off the back end, after all, especially if you haven't purchased the rights to your photos and all prints need to be ordered through the photographer.

YOU CAN OWN YOUR PHOTOS!

Some photographers, existing in a competitive market, understand the frustration of brides and grooms who pay big money for photographers to capture their wedding day, and then they have to pay big money again to buy enlargements and extra prints. So they advertise that they offer the copyright to all wedding photos. You'd pay a chunk of money to post your photos on your choice of photo developing sites. It might be the photographer's, and it might be Target or Costco, Kodak, or Shutterfly—all sources where you and your guests can buy wedding photos for a few dollars, as opposed to hundreds. Guests love being able to order prints of their own families as well as of you, and parents and grandparents say they hate it when the professional photographer's print prices are so prohibitive. So don't make the mistake of *not* asking your photographer for the rights to your photo package. And if the photographer does make his money off the back end, see if you can gain the rights to your photos after six months or so. Many experts will grant you this for a fee, and those guests who want additional photos can buy them more affordably then. You have to go by the photographer's rules, since photos on his or her site will be copy-blocked to prevent theft. They do have to make a living too.

107. Asking a friend to take the photos or video ⊘⊗⊘

No! Don't do it! Your guests don't want to work during your wedding, and that's a lot of pressure to put on a sibling, friend, or cousin. "What if the camera doesn't work?" "What if I miss an important shot?" They really sweat this volunteer job, so don't put anyone in this position unless *they* volunteer, and if they have some experience. If someone does have talent with a camera and editing, make this their wedding gift to you. But, again, don't corner a loved one and ask them to take on such an important job just to save yourself some money.

DO: Find a way to negotiate a lower-priced package with a professional photographer. They know how to get the best shots, they know how to work the lighting in the room, they have the best equipment, and they work often with budget-crunched wedding couples, so your money will be well spent.

DON'T: Skip photography and videography services, figuring that your guests will be sure to bring their own cameras, and that you can get copies of their photos and video. More and more, guests are choosing *not* to bring their own cameras to weddings due to thefts that they've read about. They don't want to leave pricy cameras at their table while they're dancing, and the photos they do take are often on their cell phones or with those throwaway cameras you'll leave on the tables. And those prints never come out all that well anyway.

108. Getting a cheesy video edit ⊘⊘

Don't pay extra so that the video editor can show off the special effects he has created or downloaded from some cliché website. You don't need strobe effects or animated characters blowing kisses from the corner of the video, cherubs flying around you and shooting arrows into you, or other nonessentials. When your videographer talks about edits, stick with the length of the video—an edited version can be about an hour for more comfortable viewing time—and tell the expert to skip the special effects. When you're paying your videographer, you're paying for his time and effort on the edit, and these special effects can add hours to your package. It's better left out.

CHAPTER 14

WEDDING GOWNS AND TUXES

*M*istakes made with your wedding gown or tuxedo are *glaringly* obvious to your guests, not to mention the fact that you'll feel awful in a gown that doesn't suit you, which makes this one of the top categories where you want to do everything as correctly as possible. So take note of the top mistakes in the wardrobe department.

GOWN MISTAKES:

109. Ordering in the size you hope to be ⊘⊘⊘

Don't tempt frustration by ordering a dress in a size 2, which is your weight-loss goal, when you are not a size 2 at the present time. So many brides "order down," thinking at this early stage of the game that needing to lose twenty pounds to get into the dress is going to be a great motivator. It only works that way about 5 percent of the time. Some brides do meet their fitness goals in time for the wedding, hopefully doing so in a healthy way, but many do not. And so they're stressed and angry and full of self-loathing, which of course leads to excess ice cream consumption, which means a new dress has to be ordered. Which would you rather experience: A fitting where the seamstress is tugging fabric across your back fat and saying, "this is so not going to work"? Or a fitting where there's three extra inches of room in the dress you bought in your current size, and the fact that you're swimming in the dress is proof of your successful efforts at losing weight and getting toned? Buying a super-small dress leads to supersized stress, so buy in your size if not a little bit larger ... in case you happen to need a few ice cream pints during the months before your wedding.

DO: Order your gown according to your professionally taken measurements, not online according to the dress size you normally wear. Designer gowns do not conform to everyday fashion sizes, so if you're a 6 in the real world, you may be an 8 in the wedding world. Or a 4. The tape measure will tell the tale.

DON'T: Buy a smaller size of dress when the site of your purchase doesn't allow returns. Many bridal shops and online stores or auction sites do not allow you to return a dress, so you'll be stuck with it.

110. **Not doing a movement test** ⊗⊗

A wedding gown has to move with you, not just look good when you're standing stick-straight with your arms hanging down. You're going to be dancing on your wedding day, sitting, standing, bending down, turning to look over your shoulder, lifting your arms to throw the bouquet. How does the dress look during each of these movements? When you bend over, do you flash the whole room? Do you have to waddle in that mermaid skirt? Can you walk up a flight of stairs? Make sure you move in every way possible, including sitting down, to make sure the dress *works* for you.

DO: Ask a volunteer to observe your movements, telling you if you have indeed flashed the room, or if the dress pulls across your thighs when you sit down.

DON'T: Count on a sales associate to advise you on this. As honest as any sales associate may be, no one has an eagle eye on this like your mother or your best friend. So bring a trusted observer.

Never buy a dress without first doing a movement test to be sure the gown is flattering while you're sitting, bending over, raising your arms to dance, even walking. The gown has to move with you and look fantastic no matter what you're doing.

iii. **Going too sexy** ⊗⊗⊗

How awful would it be if you bought your dream designer dress for $5,000, and then you found out that your house of worship does not allow bare arms or shoulders, and showing a little leg is *definitely* not allowed? Aside from taste level, some houses of worship will turn you away at the door if you're too exposed. They take their skin-baring rules seriously, and if you ignore their printed pamphlets saying so, they will not allow you to marry there. When the guests show up and you're crying on the front steps, the murmurs will be, "they said she's half naked!" You don't want that. So first, check with your house of worship about the bare shoulders rule, and clear it with them that you can wear a wrap or a stylish jacket over your strapless dress. Done. Next, challenge your personal style for form-fitting skirts, and at least try on a few A-line skirts or ballgowns, something a little more traditional and conservative. It may be your comfort level to wear tight-fitting dresses, but as we've all seen on those fashion makeover shows, you can look incredibly sexy without being too revealing.

DO: Ask the gown associate to suggest some more conservative looks if your personal style is on the more revealing side. Ask about illusion netting to cover up that deep cleavage or to cover your arms, cap sleeves to cover shoulders, or taking that leg slit down to a more appropriate height.

DON'T: Dress yourself more moderately and then allow your bridesmaids to tart themselves up with low-cut bodices and high-slit skirts. The formality of their dresses, and the decency level, has to work for them as well. There's a mistake lurking in this issue as well ... how do you tell your bridesmaid not to dress too sexy without her assuming that you're saying she *always* dresses inappropriately? Some bridesmaids are quick to take offense at anything, not wanting to be judged—especially if she is envious of all your good fortune these days—so your innocent comment of "it's a conservative church, so make sure your dress is not too revealing" can turn into a battle royale, the silent treatment, and a quickfire "can you believe what she said to me?" gossip frenzy among the bridesmaids. So when you have *any* concerns about a bridesmaid's sexpot level of dressing, send a group e-mail to *all* of the bridesmaids, with the same message. That hypersensitive bridesmaid, then, can't enjoy the drama of it being all about her.

112. Ordering from a disreputable place to save money ✒

Where you buy your gown is almost as important as which gown you buy. So be sure that you're shopping at a boutique that has been around for a long time—as opposed to a gown shop that *just* opened in town, since those may be of the variety to take your deposit and disappear the next week. Ask your friends for referrals to where they bought their wedding gowns or formal dresses, and even if the prices are slightly higher, count it as an investment in making this most important purchase from a shop that values quality and customer service. Word-of-mouth referrals are always far superior to those online reviews you'll find ... some of which may be glowing reviews written by the owner under an alias or raves written by all of her friends. Depend on your most trusted companions to direct you to the perfect gown shop or designer's atelier.

> Don't order your dress from a gown shop that *just* opened in town, since those may be of the variety to take your deposit and disappear the next week.

113. Ordering before you have chosen your wedding style and season ⊘⊘⊘

Granted, most dresses can be worn in any season, so the month of your eventual wedding date may only cause an issue if you want a brocade or heavier fabric gown for a spring or summer wedding. It's more the formality of the wedding that matters here—if you buy an informal gown and then change your wedding plans to a formal wedding, you're going to look out of place. The same goes for your new destination wedding plans, where you'll get winded dragging around a five-foot train on the pink sand beaches of Bermuda.

DO: Research gowns to your heart's content, but buy only once you're sure of your wedding's season, formality, style, and location.

DON'T: Try to wear a winter gown in summertime. The weight of the dress and the wintry accents will be a dead giveaway that you mismatched your dress and your wedding date.

114. Not getting a good seamstress ⊘⊘⊘

A talented seamstress is the *best* investment you can make in how you'll look on your wedding day. Gowns hang differently on different body shapes, and the trained eye (and hand) of a quality seamstress can not only make the gown look magnificent on you, but can often create the illusion of weight loss! A shoddy seamstress, or a do-it-yourself attempt at taking in seams and fitting bodices, shows like a beacon. The dress doesn't move with you. The top is too tight, or it sags. Hems come loose during the dancing hours. All because you wanted to save a few bucks. Ask around and employ the services of the best seamstress out there to bring out the magic of the gown you've so lovingly chosen.

WHERE TO FIND A GOOD SEAMSTRESS

Most bridal gown shops employ their own talented team of seamstresses, and alterations may be included in the price of your dress. If, however, you're not buying your dress at a bridal salon, you'll need to locate the best independent seamstress out there. Ask at gown shops, since many feature the business cards of their favorite freelance seamstresses right there by the cash register; ask recently married friends for referrals to the experts they used; and check in at *tailoring* shops! I've found that the best tailors, often fifth-generation businesses, excel at altering wedding gowns, and I've personally had a tailor hand-create a corset effect for the back of a bridesmaid dress that arrived too small. The result was amazing and the price was lower because the shop was not in the bridal business. It's worth checking out.

115. Ordering bridesmaids' dresses online without research first ⊘⊗⊘

Before your bridesmaids click in their dress orders, make sure you've carefully researched the department store or designer's website to find out their returns policy. Do they give a full refund within thirty days? Do they only give store credit in return? Are sale-priced gowns nonreturnable? Even though it's your bridesmaids' order to make, you can prevent several big mistakes, and group anger, by investigating the site or calling customer service to inquire about returns and exchanges rules.

TUXEDO MISTAKES:

116. Getting the cheapest style ⊘⊘⊘

"But we're only going to wear it once!" The grooms and the men may balk at the heightened prices of attractive designer label tuxedoes, especially when they see the basic tuxes for $30 or less. It's a huge mistake to rent the cheap suits. Your men have different body types, and we now live in an era where people know good men's fashion from bad. We've all seen George Clooney on a red carpet, after all. And the men want to look like that. The wedding guests notice when the men don't look like that. Why pay more for a designer brand (think Armani) tux? It's about fit. And fabric. And quality of workmanship. Those bargain-priced tuxes are fine for proms, but this is your wedding. So if your groom has taken on the task of choosing the tuxedo style for himself, his men, the dads, and the ringbearers, make sure you've educated him about how a quality tux is the better investment.

DO: Go with him to check out the selection, and invite the tuxedo salesperson to give a little lecture about the differences in fabrics for weight, breatheability, sheen, and construction. Grooms tend to honor the authority figure in the tux shop, especially when you're presented with different tuxes to feel.

DON'T: Send him an article about tuxedo jacket cuts, focusing only on the right style for your wedding formality, without focusing on fabric and coordinating vests, ties, and shirts. Even if men are fashion-savvy, the details of tuxedo world can often overwhelm them. Be involved, be present, be informative, but let your groom make the final choice from a selection of quality tuxes.

117. **Men sending their sizes without being measured** ◎◎◎

Men who have never been in a bridal party before may not be aware that when a tux is ordered, the sizing depends on their *exact* measurements for neck, chest, arm length, inseam, and other vital data. So don't let them call in guesses at their neck size according to what kind of business shirts they wear. Some men wear the wrong size every day. Send them a detailed e-mail explaining that they have to go to a tailor or tux rental shop to get their measurements professionally taken and recorded on a size card, and then they need to send that size card to you either in the mail or via an e-mail.

DO: Offer to pay for their measurements to be taken. Some shops charge for the time needed by the tailor to take the half-dozen different measurements, especially when that's the only service you require of them.

DON'T: Leave this task for the last minute. Give them a good month to get their sizes in before their deposits and order are due. Also, don't take measurements from them right before the winter holidays. Tux rental experts say that they ask their clients to wait until after they gain their 5 pounds from holiday meals and New Year's celebrations.

KEEP TRACK OF YOUR MEN SENDING THEIR SIZE CARDS

Use this space to check off each man (including fathers and ringbearers) who has sent in his size card and who hasn't (yet). These are the tiny details that can fall through the cracks when you don't write them down, causing untold headaches and expensive rush orders for all later on:

NAME	SENT
_____	☐
_____	☐
_____	☐
_____	☐
_____	☐
_____	☐
_____	☐
_____	☐

118. Using prom-like colors ◎◎

Where have you seen photos of a woman in a pink dress and a man in a matching pink vest and tie? The prom. Leave that look to the kids, and class it up with blacks, grays, and whites for a formal wedding. You can, of course, choose colored or patterned vests or colored long ties for the men if that's your chosen style for the wedding, but that look works best in deeper, richer colors like burgundies rather than pastels like lavender, pink, and baby blue.

119. **Not having a tux return plan** *⁊*

It can cost each of your men a few hundred dollars if their tuxedoes and rented accessories like shoes are not returned to the store by noon the next day. And if a man has lost his vest, tie, or jacket, that's going to be a hefty replacement cost. So even though the last thing on anyone's mind on the night of the wedding is organizing each man's outfit for a timely return the next morning, that's exactly what you must arrange. Pre-arrange, actually. Tell the guys, and have a responsible male in the circle remind them, to hang their jackets, pants, vests, ties, and other items in their garment bags—hopefully with each man using the garment bag labeled with his name—and hand them off to the designated collector. Fathers of the bride or groom often agree to assume this role, with a prearranged collection place and time set and reminded on the day of the wedding. It might be the night before, when everyone changes out of their formalwear into clubbing clothes for the after-party, or it might be at a decent hour (10 A.M.) on the morning after the wedding. The collector gets the group's tux bags and shoes, and runs the entire order back to the tux rental shop in time to prevent any second-day charges.

DO: Ask the tux rental place if you can have a 3 P.M. return time. Most places will accommodate you, and many hotels will gladly send their concierges to each groomsmen's room to collect the tux packages.

DON'T: Forget to remind the men on the morning and evening of the wedding about the tux return plan. Some couples tell the guys' wives or girlfriends as backup reminder sources.

It can cost each of your men a few hundred dollars if their tuxedoes and rented accessories like shoes are not returned to the store by noon the next day.

120. Not having a men's socks and accessories plan ⊘⊘⊘

There's always going to be the guy who wears white socks with black dress shoes. So make sure your men are advised about wearing black socks, make sure they all have identical ties—don't just say, "go get a black tie"—and make sure your groom or one of the other men can advise on button covers and cufflinks. The details are important to the uniformity of the men's classic looks, even if they're not going to be in tuxedos! If you love the look of khaki pants and crisp white shirts, that too has to be a uniformly purchased outfit. Khaki can range from beige to a light green, and white dress shirts can differ as well. So that means a group shopping trip for the men to buy matching outfit pieces and accessories.

DO: Ask the men to allow you an advance look at their wedding-day shoes if they won't be renting them. Yes, they'll call you a control freak, but this is the only way to ensure you won't have a groomsman with brown dress shoes with his black tux.

DON'T: Let the groom talk you out of checking on these details. Of course he doesn't want to get teased by his friends, but if you calmly explain that you're looking out for *them*, that you don't want them to feel uncomfortable in those brown shoes, your groom may get on board, or encourage you to funnel your request through the best man instead of calling his guys yourself. Whatever works.

CHAPTER 15

FLOWERS AND DÉCOR

*M*istakes with flowers might not affect your wedding as mightily as mistakes with your budget, or
with people, but missteps here can take some of the shine off
of your perfect wedding vision. Imagine seeing your groom for
the first time, and he has no boutonniere because the florist
left it at his house instead of delivering it to the hotel where he
and the guys were getting ready. None of the men have flowers on their lapels! It's not a catastrophe, but it is one of those
things that guests notice and that raise your pulse when you're
plucking a rose out of your bouquet and fastening it to your
groom's tux minutes before the photos are taken.

Since you're not likely to be an expert in all things floral,
the following tips will prevent you from making the most
common flower-centric mistakes that happen at *other* people's
weddings all too often.

121. Choosing flowers that need a water source ⊘

Some flowers, like hydrangeas, need a water source for the length of the day, or else they quickly wilt. That's why few floral designers will choose this particular type of flower for a mom's wristlet or corsage. An hour into the day Mom's wristlet is going to turn brown and fall apart. It's a mistake to assume that all flowers will last throughout the day, keeping their shape and color even in the hot summer sun. Different varieties of flowers have different tolerance levels for heat and different needs for moisture, and some flower petals—such as gardenias—are known for speeding up their aging process if they come into contact with the oils of your fingers. So make sure that you ask your floral designer about the blooms' need for water, any no-touch rules, or other instructions to ensure longevity and freshness throughout the timeline of your day.

122. Choosing too big or heavy a bouquet ⊘⊘

It looked great in the picture, but it weighs twenty pounds. A big, dramatic bouquet with dozens of flowers tightly arranged, plus a sturdy handle, can be quite heavy. Some brides find themselves struggling to keep that bouquet upright with one hand while they take their father's arm for the walk down the aisle. "It hurts my wrist!" one bride complained to her floral designer right before the wedding, and nothing could be done at that point to remove some of the heft. Consider weight as well as size and appearance, because you'll be holding that bouquet up for the ceremony and for photos, and your maid of honor will have to hold your heavy bouquet as well as her own during the ring portion of your ceremony! It would be a big mistake for you to have sore wrists or not be willing to hold those beautiful bouquets for very long.

DO: Ask your floral designer if you can come in to "test hold" a few different bouquets. You may decide to scale down your design for greater comfort. Also, show your floral designer a photo of your gown so that you can choose a bouquet style that's most in symmetry with the gown and with your body shape and size.

DON'T: Saddle your bridesmaids with heavy bouquets. No matter the size of yours, make theirs smaller as a uniform visual effect and as a way to save some money.

It would be a big mistake for you to have sore wrists or not be willing to hold those beautiful bouquets for very long.

123. **Choosing flowers that aren't suitable for your allergies** ⊘⊗⊘

I asked a floral designer which flowers would work best for my own allergies, and she said, "oh, most flowers are about the same." Oh, *really?* Then why am I sneezing and wheezing while I'm standing near an arrangement on my friend's dining room table? The truth is that some flowers create less pollen and therefore have less of an effect on allergy sufferers. Trumpet-shaped flowers like calla lilies and daffodils are among the most allergy-friendly because their pollen stays inside the flower itself. Some experts say that brightly colored flowers are a great bet. If you suffer from allergies, ask your florist if you can try out the different flowers he or she has in mind for your bouquet and your centerpieces—grooms should try out their boutonniere flowers if they have allergies as well—to see how you tolerate the pollen. This is a matter of making an appointment with your florist so that you can spend a bit of time near the flowers. Or, find a great nursery where you can linger near the freesia, ranunculus, roses, and especially the ornamental grasses, like Bermuda grass, which often surprises many brides and grooms with their potent effects. You don't want allergies to congest you or make your eyes all red and puffy, cause a sneezing fit, or make your throat itchy during your wedding day, so plan ahead for a floral test, and ask your bridal party members to do the same before you place your order. Bridal party members will appreciate your e-mail saying "please let us know if you have any allergies to flowers!"

124. Not checking with the moms for their choices of floral pieces ⊘⊘

It sounds like a no-brainer, but you wouldn't believe the number of bride-mom skirmishes that happen because the bride chose the type of flower she wanted both mothers to wear. Don't try to make the moms (and stepmoms) into a matching set with their flowers. Allow them to choose their own favorite flowers, and whether they wish to wear a corsage or have a wristlet. This is one area where the moms should have their say.

DO: Include stepmothers, godmothers, grandmothers, the parents of the child attendants, and perhaps even the officiant in your personal flower order. It would be a mistake to leave these women out of the honor, even if you're on a budget. Your floral designer can create lovely little inexpensive pieces for them.

DON'T: Be afraid of big wristlets or corsages, thinking they're too 1980s. Today's floral designers are showing more dramatic pieces, so it's truly the mom's choice of which style she wants.

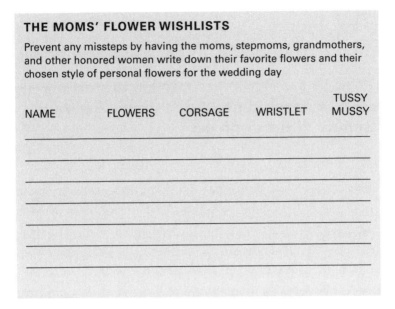

125. **Not having a floral delivery and setup plan** ⊘⊘⊘

Make sure you give your floral designer *detailed* instructions on where each set of bouquets and boutonnieres are to be delivered, so that nothing is lost and no member of your bridal party is left without a bouquet or boutonniere. Delivery problems have sent bridesmaids down the aisle without flowers, even the *bride* down the aisle without flowers, because the big box of blooms was sent to the wrong place. If you're at your house and your groom is at a hotel room, then your separate flower deliveries have to be organized and delivered on time. Write out a checklist of what needs to go where, from the ceremony site to the reception site, and for each location, give the designer a written description of the placement you have in mind. It might read like this: "Floral arch is to be set five feet behind the altar; pew decorations go on the first three rows of each side, with the pink-flowered ones affixed to the first rows; entrance floral décor is to be placed on the grand piano, not on the glass table to the side." And so on. You can't be too detailed with your descriptions. Floral designers *want* these details, because they don't want you to come crying to them because you had to stand *under* the arch, not in front of it.

DO: Draw up sketches, if you have to. These help not just the floral designer, but his or her assistants.

DON'T: Order décor for looks alone without any thought to where they will go. The floral designer will place them for you, as will volunteers if you don't hire a floral designer to deliver your order or if you're going all do-it-yourself with your décor, but then you're stuck with someone else's décor vision.

126. Not checking about existing décor and what you can bring in ✗

Always ask the site manager for a list of don'ts as decreed by the establishment. Some sites won't allow tents to be staked into the ground. They won't allow candles without hurricane lamps, as a matter of their insurance policy. They won't allow potted plants on the grounds because they don't want their lawn to develop dark circles or grass damage. No tiki torches. No floral garlands hung on the banisters, no floral décor on their chandeliers. If you purchase these things and they arrive to a big "no" on the wedding day, that's thousands of dollars wasted. Make the call and check first. Don't take a floral designer's word that she's worked at that site before ... management might have changed since then, with new rules enforced.

CHAPTER 16

INVITATIONS

Invitations are the number-one wedding category where mistakes are made due to etiquette rules. Traditional etiquette still holds true to Old-World standards of what's proper and what's not. The invitations arrive in all of your guests' mailboxes as the big announcement of your big day, and they convey so much more than the actual words you have printed on them. The list of invitation-wording rules is long (such as "no abbreviations" and "use the titles of Miss for girls and Master for boys"), so I've listed the top five mistakes to help you avoid the biggest offenses that guests and parents take *really* seriously.

127. Not listing the parents' names when they're paying for the wedding ⊘⊘⊘

The parents are going to be irate when they see that their names are not on the invitation, and they won't take "the designer said there was no room" as an excuse. Yes, we know it can be difficult to get multiple sets of parents' names on an invitation when you have divorced and remarried parents in your inner circle, but that's why they invented tri-panel invitations. When parents are paying for all or *part* of the wedding—even if you're kicking in the majority of cash— they should have their names on the invitation. It means a great deal to them. So if you're worried about having enough space on your invitation for all of those names—which can be up to six lines in some cases!—choose a tri-fold invitation that allows you to devote a whole panel to the honor of listing them. It also helps some guests recognize who *you* are if they're among your parents' colleagues, friends, and others from the guest list.

128. Not conveying the formality with your wording ⊘

Guests want to know if this will be a formal wedding so that they know how to dress. Even with today's more relaxed standards when it comes to wording invitations—some couples wish to be more conversational and more "them" in their invites—it's a mistake to go too casual with your wording. Save that for the prewedding parties, showers, bachelorette's party invitations, and wedding breakfast invitations. The *wedding* invitation is still a place for formal wording rules if you'll have a formal wedding.

LOOK UP WORDING EXAMPLES

On invitation websites, you'll find countless sample phrasings to suit an array of family situations, such as a departed parent, divorced parents, formal invitation wording, response cards, and so on. Use those as your model, and talk with your invitation specialist about font sizing and arrangement on the panels.

129. Misspelling a guest's name, or not including their title, on the envelope ⊘⊗⊘

Yikes, there's just no excuse for that! Check with parents and other friends to make sure you have the correct spelling, *all* of their kids' names (they may have had a baby in the years since you saw them last) if the kids are invited, and honor their title if they are a judge, attorney, captain, military servicemember, pastor, and so on. You *can* call them directly to check—they love it that you respect the position they've attained in life.

130. Putting gift registry information on the invitation ⊘⊗⊘

That's a big etiquette don't. Registry information can go on your personalized wedding website and in shower invitations, but never on wedding invitations . . . not even informal ones.

You *can* enclose a card with your wedding website, though. They'll find out your registry info along with their travel and hotel info.

Registry information can go on your personalized wedding website and in shower invitations, but never on wedding invitations . . . not even informal ones.

131. Putting "and guest" when the recipient is in a long-term relationship or is engaged ⊗⊗⊗

Again, this is a research thing, and an essential step to make sure you don't offend both the guest and his or her partner. People get very upset over this one, and when they call your parents about it, that's an even bigger problem because now your parents are embarrassed. Guests somehow feel that parents should have known and advised you better.

DO: Find out the names of your guests' guests—you can call them directly if you have never known their significant other's name, or ask a friend or relative for the info.

DON'T: Take chances in guessing at a guest's boyfriend's name . . . because she might not have the same boyfriend you remember. He might be her ex now.

CHAPTER 17

TRANSPORTATION AND LODGING

In this section, we're focusing on the steps you need to take before you book those limousines or arrange for your guests' hotel room block. Previous brides and grooms have spent their money unwisely because they weren't aware of smarter options, and their guests wound up with everything from lumpy mattresses to paper-thin walls (who needs to hear *that* going on next door) to bugbites. So take these warnings into account, because the mistakes made in this category can be extremely upsetting.

132. Having the limousines wait during the reception ✗

The wedding packages you see at the limousine companies mean that you're paying for the minute the cars leave the lot, as they take you to the ceremony, wait for the ceremony to be over (perhaps an hour), take you to the reception, then wait outside the reception hall for the end of the party when they take you to your hotel. And you're paying hourly! Save yourselves a few hours of running meter by ending the limousine's service when they drop you at the reception hall. You can arrange for another ride to your hotel, perhaps a free ride if you hop on the hotel shuttle taking all of the guests to that same hotel. Or, just arrange for pickup and dropoff service with a limousine company. Yes, you can venture off of the wedding package to just hire them for two separate trips.

DO: Check into regular pickup and dropoff rates at any limousine or classic car companies, or have a responsible, sober friend drive you to your hotel in their car (perhaps a convertible decorated with a "just married" sign).

DON'T: Pay for all of those hours just to have the limo sit in a parking lot while you're inside partying.

133. Not prearranging your luggage to be sent where you're going ◌◌

Don't start your wedding night off with a ride back to your house to get your luggage, or suffer the stress of not knowing where your luggage is! This is one of those things that slips brides' and grooms' minds in the hectic pace of the wedding morning. But it won't happen to *you* because you have this book. Save yourself the need to drive back to your place to retrieve your suitcase and carryon (and passport) by assigning a volunteer to make sure your luggage is in the trunk of your car or brought to your honeymoon suite on the morning of the wedding. Triple-check to make sure you have everything you need, especially if your honeymoon flight is first thing in the morning the next day.

DO: Make sure you're aware of the acceptable size measurements for carryon bags, as mandated by your airline carrier. Visit their website to get the length-by-width-by-height numbers and measure your own baggage, even if you've flown recently and never had a problem. With some honeymoon packages that send you on a different airline, the rules may be different, and you want to avoid the last-minute stress of having to check your carryon bags as well as your suitcases.

DON'T: Assume you can carry anything on board the plane. Triple check the new guidelines for what's allowed on board, how cosmetics and liquids need to be packaged, and which unusual things are now considered weapons. For instance, that bottle of wine that someone gave you for your first toast on your honeymoon—you might have to throw that out because it's not allowed on the plane.

Don't start your wedding night off with a ride back to your house to get your luggage, or suffer the stress of not knowing where your luggage is!

134. **Not arranging for the free hotel shuttle and not knowing the rules for it** ⊗⊗⊗

Don't miss out on a perk, or allow your guests to stress about renting cars to get around town (at even more expense, just to attend your wedding). Most hotels in major chains offer the use of their shuttle bus for *free*, as a way for your guests to get to and from the ceremony and the reception. All you have to do is talk to the sales manager. This is a perk they give to wedding couples, sometimes even if you're not holding your reception in their ballroom! It's often enough that you book your hotel room block there. So you have to book those rooms soon and reserve the use of the shuttle bus soon, or else other wedding couples could take your freebie! When you ask—and you do have to ask for this service—find out where else your guests may be able to take the shuttle. It could transport them to and from the airport or train station, or to local malls for shopping trips, or to churches and synagogues for worship services. All for free. So check ahead on this great service for your guests, and make sure you know their allotted schedule. For instance, the hotel may agree to offer one trip to your ceremony site, departing at noon on the dot. And it may offer shuttle trips home from the reception every half hour starting at 9 P.M. but only lasting until 11 P.M. Print up these rules for insertion in your out-of-town guests' welcome baskets so that they know how to arrange their own timing.

135. Saying you'll leave early ✄

When you book your limousine, you'll be asked what time you want to leave your reception so that the limo is ready and waiting for you. If, at this early stage of the game, you see an early departure as a way to save money, you might sign a contract saying that you'll be picked up at 11 P.M. But what happens if the party is in full swing at 11 P.M. and you don't want to leave? Or, if you don't notice the time until midnight? You're going to pay hefty overtime fees. And if you decide during the course of your reception that a group of you would like to go out for an after-party, you can tell the limo driver to go back to home base . . . but you're still going to pay for the hours you reserved. So if you do choose to have a limo waiting for you at the end of the reception, pick a realistic departure time, knowing that brides and grooms stay until the end of the reception now.

136. Not seeing a hotel room before arranging the room block ⊗⊗⊗

You've found two hotels that are close to the reception hall. One is a little bit expensive, and the other is more moderately priced. You've seen the hotel website, like the amenities, and the price range is suitable for your guests. But have you toured the hotel and taken a look at a room? You absolutely must, since you don't want your guests to spend the night in a seedy dump with poor quality sheets, bad plumbing, the sounds of a super-highway right outside their bedroom window, or the thumping bass of the nightclub right next door . . . or that sickening chlorine smell from an indoor pool. Ask the sales manager to show you a selection of rooms before you sign a contract or post the room block information on your wedding website, just to make sure it's a place that you would want to stay.

DO: Make an appointment for a tour, and ask to see several rooms—not just the one the manager takes you to.

DON'T: Trust the reviews you see on travel websites. See the rooms in person. And don't book a room block at any hotel where the manager says they don't do room tours. That's never a good sign.

You absolutely must see guest hotel rooms in person, since you don't want your guests to spend the night in a seedy dump with poor quality sheets, bad plumbing, or the sounds of a super-highway right outside their bedroom window.

CHAPTER 18

FAVORS AND GIFTS

*W*hile this isn't the most controversial of subjects, you can take a few careful steps to make sure that the items you choose to give will be received well. The favors are the last accent that wedding guests see on the big day, so this is an opportunity to make a great choice and thank your guests for attending right in the moment.

137. Having no favors ◎◎◎

For a short time in the quickly changing whims of wedding world, brides and grooms opted not to give out favors as a way to save money. "Who needs another little silver frame?" was the battle cry of those who chose to go without. But with the advent of attractive and useful favors in affordable price ranges, and with our wonderful return to etiquette-over-dollars, brides and grooms once again enjoy the task of choosing great favors and packaging them to suit their wedding's theme, colors, and their own personalities. Why miss out on a chance to give your guests an extra little something sweet and adorable, and thereby make *yourselves* look like a generous, thoughtful couple? It would be a big mistake to give nothing, since guests know that the trend is to offer a small favor, often an edible favor, and they have received lovely items like these at other weddings. They will notice the absence of favors, and that's a bad last impression for your wedding day. It shows that you tried to save money, and it gives the impression that you don't care enough to send them off well, since you have their wedding gift in hand now.

138. Making a donation to a controversial charity ⊘⊗⊘

In the past few years, it's become a big trend for wedding couples to make a donation to their favorite charity in lieu of giving favors. Guests would get a pretty printed card, perhaps with a candy attached, bearing the announcement that "A donation has been made to [charity]," perhaps in the name of a departed relative or friend. It's a very nice tribute, and guests have been pleased to know the couple's generosity extends to giving back to the world. Where the mistake comes into play is if the charity in question is one of political or activist interest. While you may believe strongly in your political party of choice, or an animal rights group or extremist environmental group, your guests might have strong feelings about that particular affiliation. So steer clear of any charities that stir up controversy on the news, research your contenders well at *www.justgive.org* or *www.idofoundation.org*, and choose a charity that does good work in an area that's important to all.

When donating to charity, steer clear of any charities that stir up controversy.

139. Giving different favors according to a favoritism plan ⊘⊘⊘

This one *really* angers guests. The bride and groom walk around the room giving little favor boxes to their college friends, their colleagues, and their cousins, and then they walk around giving out *bigger* favor boxes to relatives and parents' friends who they know were able to give larger cash wedding gifts. Guests should never be gifted according to financial brackets! So choose one lovely favor style that everyone will receive just the same.

DO: Give those larger thank-you gifts to wedding contributors and guests who allowed you to use their home, car, or contacts at another time, perhaps at the rehearsal dinner.

DON'T: Confuse gifts with favors. Gifts are given outside of visual range of all the wedding guests.

140. **Giving a favor that guests can't get home** ⊘⊘

With the strict rules in airline travel that have all of us trans-porting our contact lens solution and shampoo in little bottles, sealed in regulation plastic bags, a favor in any form of liq-uid or even candle might not be allowed on the plane ride home. Airport screeners regularly make passengers throw out expensive face creams and pampering lotions. So those guests will have to leave their favors behind. Take guests' travel into consideration, including those who will be driving home ... a liquid or favor that needs to be refrigerated (like a slice of wedding cake) might not make the trip with them.

DO: Give an edible favor like a box of truffles, which is often enjoyed right after (or during) the reception if you have any question about travel safety.

DON'T: Give plants or seedlings, herbs, or wine bottle stop-pers with pointy edges. All of these will be confiscated by air-line security.

141. **Giving personalized guest welcome baskets** ⊘⊘

When guests check into their hotel rooms, they'll be thrilled to find a welcome basket from you. Inside, there are bottles of water, soda, a bottle of wine, chocolates, snacks, the itinerary for the wedding weekend, and more goodies like pampering products. The mistake here is in personalizing the bags with guests' names and expecting hotel personnel to deliver the right bag to the right hotel room. Most hotels add on an extra charge for that! So avoid the mistake of having to pay more by making all the bags identical for easier placement in hotel rooms.

CHAPTER 19

WEDDING-DAY BEAUTY AND COMFORT

There are some *big* mistakes you can make when it comes to your wedding day look. Frosted eyeshadow. Fake-a-bake tanning the day before the wedding, to the point where you're so burned you can't even smile. Glitter all over your cleavage. Beauty experts second the wisdom that you should keep your look natural, like you, only better. So avoid the following mistakes so that you don't wreck your look . . . and your day.

142. Going too dramatic with the makeup ◎◎◎

Many brides think that in order to look great in their photographs, they have to intensify their makeup application, much like an actor does on stage. Eye makeup is darkened, lips are cherry red, blush is a streak along the cheekbone. And foundation is *thick*. But that isn't the case. You need to look great *in person* more so than in the photographs, so depend on the services of a great makeup professional who knows the perfect application touch for your cosmetics to make you look great in person and on film. Too many brides attempt to save money by doing their own makeup on the wedding day, and that can be an option *if* you've first gone for a trial makeup application lesson with a pro. For less than $35 in most cases, a makeup stylist will teach you how to accent your eyes and smooth that foundation, remove the shine and have a softer look overall. So even if you're short on cash, you can still avoid the mistakes made by inexperienced brides who think they should just slap on another few coats of mascara and darken their eyebrows with a liner pencil. Don't go for a Halloween effect. Put your face in the hands of a professional.

143. Getting a facial or other procedure right before the wedding ◌◌◌

This is the number-one mistake that can be made in this category. You want to look beautiful, soft, and natural on your wedding day, not red-faced, peeling, broken out, or sunburned. When you think that being the bride-to-be means you should go for special face treatments as a VIP treat, *never* do so a week or two right before the wedding. Especially with facials and skin peels—you don't know how your skin is going to react. Some people have such sensitive skin that they get very burned, their face breaks out, or they break capillaries on their cheeks and nose. Some brides who go to inexperienced aestheticians wind up with permanent scarring when the treatment is not done correctly or when their skin is just too sensitive for the harsh chemicals and abrasive treatments. So if you want to explore the effects of facials or chemical peels, do so as far before the wedding as possible to see how they work for you. Watch those inevitable healing days afterward to keep track of how long you're red, how much you peel, and how uncomfortable it is to smile or talk or chew. The same goes for tanning, whether you wish to apply self-tanner, go to a tanning salon, or bake in your backyard. We all know that tanning can be dangerous, so it's wise to practice good health measures by avoiding UV rays as much as possible. For any skin-coloring treatment like self-tanning lotions or spray-on tans, again, try this out as far before the wedding as possible to see if you look orange, if the tanner comes off on your clothes or sheets, if it burns or stings after application, or any other side effect that would make you unhappy on your wedding day.

DO: See what a makeup artist can do with your existing skin tone, rather than feel like you have to have a bronze celebrity tan on your wedding day. Countless brides look at their wedding photos and wonder why they ever thought they'd look good with a deep, deep tan. "I didn't match my husband!" says one recent bride whose wedding-day tan was so brown that her fiancé looked pale and anemic standing next to her. Other brides complained of having orange-stained hands from trying to do their own self-tanning applications.

DON'T: Take on any skin-altering treatment yourself, and don't go to a pro for the first time within weeks of your wedding.

It would be a shame for you to hate the way you look . . . or for you to look cartoonish to your guests.

If you want to explore the effects of facials, chemical peels, or self-tanners, do so as far before the wedding as possible to see how they work for you.

144. Wearing false eyelashes you're not used to ⊗⊗⊗

False eyelashes are all the rage with brides who want to look gorgeous on the wedding day. Celebrities wear them. We see them in magazine beauty features. We see those little packages of faux eyelashes on the racks in beauty supply stores, and the directions on the box make it sound so easy! But applying a thin little line of *glue* to your eyelid, and then applying the thin strip of eyelash—which you have to cut to the ideal length of your eye—and then applying liquid liner over the seam to cover the glue marks . . . that's nearly an impossible task, and few women can master this without tons and tons of practice. So a beginner's attempt should never be a wedding-day look. You run the risk of an uneven lash line, lashes that are too bushy for your eyes, liner smears, glue in your eye, lashes that don't take and flutter every time you blink. Not to mention that it can feel strange to have something foreign on your eyes, making you blink more rapidly. And no bride wants to hear, "you have a caterpillar on your cheek" when the lash falls off while greeting guests.

DO: Visit a beauty salon for a practice application of false eyelashes. Models suggest that you have individual lashes applied, not full strips. A pro can apply the perfect length of lashes to the perfect spots on your eyeline, and the quality of the false lashes they have far surpasses anything you'd find in a pharmacy beauty aisle. So if mascara is not enough of an effect for you, look into an expert application of lashes both in a trial run and on the wedding day.

DON'T: Goop on a poor quality mascara in too dark a shade to give the effect of false eyelashes. That too can be a disaster, especially if the tears start flowing during your ceremony, or if it's a hot day that can cause your eye makeup to run. Your eyes need to shine on the wedding day, so make sure they catch attention for their sparkle, not for the hideous hairy things above them or the spiky mascara job you did yourself.

145. **Wearing troublesome undergarments** ◌

The right undergarments make your gown look amazing, and can make you look ten pounds thinner. From body slimmers to control top pantyhose to pushup bras, strapless bras, and corsets, what you wear under your dress can be just as important as the dress itself. So brides are investing an impressive amount of money in the best undergarments possible. The *mistake*, however, is in choosing the wrong style or size and dealing with pinching or shifting undergarments, control tops that roll down and make a tire effect across your middle, or an ill-fitting bra that means you're tugging at your bodice all night. The grievous error is not testing your undergarments well before the big day. They are quite literally the foundation of your look—so pantylines are out of the question!—and bad choices will have you fidgeting in noticeable discomfort all night long.

DO: Visit specialty undergarment stores such as Bra Smyth or other upscale shops that will *measure* you to find or custom-create the perfect undergarments for your wedding day. Many brides will bring their wedding gowns to these stores for an even more detailed creation. You may find that you're not actually a 32B but are rather a 34C, and that bra's fit makes all the difference in your wedding-day look. You may try on a slimmer that reduces the silhouette of your hips, making that sheath dress look even better. This is the best shopping trip possible to make the most of your gown investment, and feeling comfortable on your wedding day is priceless.

DON'T: Give in to the "it's better to look good than feel good" mindset. If you wear, for instance, a corset that's supertight in order to give the illusion that you have a smaller waist, here's what's going to happen:

- You're going to have a hard time breathing, which could lead you to pass out.
- You're going to have a hard time eating, and since you can't loosen the corset, you'll miss out on the luscious desserts, or perhaps most of your meal.
- Guests who hug you or dance with you will be able to *feel* the boning of the corset, which could be a turnoff to your groom as well. One groom said, "It felt like her skin was sausaging out between those hard lines. It didn't feel like her, and I just knew she was in pain."
- Chafing from a too-tight undergarment can cause lasting damage to your skin, so wearing your regular bras or your bathing suit during your honeymoon is going to be painful if not impossible. Some brides have had to bandage their rubbed-raw backs and hips.
- Your focus will be on your discomfort, not on your groom or on your wedding. It would be a shame if you were counting the minutes until you could get out of there.

146. **Forgetting to do touchups** ⊘⊘⊘

You looked lovely at the ceremony, but now, three hours later, you look like you've been dipped in oil with all that shine on your nose and forehead. You have icky black mascara goop in the corners of your eyes, and your lipstick has worn away, leaving you with pale, dry lips. That's quite an image, isn't it? It's a major mistake to forget that touchups are essential for your wedding day look, since you want to look fresh all day long.

DO: Assign a bridesmaid to be on shine alert duty, meaning that she'll discreetly let you know when it's time to join her in a trip to the ladies room, where you'll powder away that shine, redo your lipstick and gloss and—very important—pop a breath mint. Plan to freshen up every hour, especially in warm weather or if you're dancing a lot.

DON'T: Forget to pack an emergency bag that contains what *you* will need. We've all seen those online articles suggesting an emery board and a sewing kit, and those lists often leave out the items that you can use most. Like oil blotting papers or a mosquito bite stick, contact lens solution and an extra pair of lenses, an EpiPen if you have allergies, a cell phone charger, moisturizing lotion, a stick of deodorant, comfort gel pads for inside your shoes, and especially the makeup products you'll need that day.

It's a major mistake to forget that touchups are essential for your wedding day look, since you want to look fresh all day long.

147. Wearing the wrong shoes for the terrain ⊘⊘⊘

Don't pick out your shoes before you know the ground you'll walk on! Brides who buy their wedding dresses and shoes before they choose a location invite disaster when their tiny little stiletto heels are no match for marble terraces that are slick from the rain, cobblestone pathways, or damp grass (heels sink right in, and down you go!). Brides who wear delicate, high-heeled shoes in outdoor settings are the first to turn an ankle or take a tumble, which is never a joyous moment for any bride on her wedding day. Especially if it's the beginning of the party and you injure your foot, keeping you from dancing, or if you have to endure comments of "she's drunk already" from that obnoxious uncle or your sister's husband, who will remind you of this moment at every family holiday. Enjoy your shoe shopping trip! Choosing shoes has become an exciting part of the fashion celebration for your big day, but make sure that you know about slatted terraces, cobblestone walkways, wooden paths to the beach, and other terrain challenges before you spend hundreds on that great pair of wedding-day shoes.

DO: Try on shoes with wider heels. They're still pretty, but they give you a little bit more support and don't sink into damp grass or sand like stilettos do.

DON'T: Feel like you have to wear clunky, chunky shoes that don't match your dress and don't make you feel fabulous. And don't buy shoes that hurt when you put them on ... you'll be standing in these shoes for *hours* on the wedding day, so you want all straps to feel natural, no rubs, no irritation, no little toes curled under and throbbing already. Buying ill-fitting shoes and—again—walking into that mantra of it being better to look good than to feel good is just foolish. Everyone can tell if you're unsteady on your heels, and physical pain is not part of your wedding dream.

148. Having no jackets or wrap ⊗⊗

You might think that this is just a winter and early fall issue, but you'd be surprised how breezy and chilly it can get after a summer's rain, or at the beach after sundown. There's *no* season that's out of season for a great jacket or wrap to coordinate with your wedding gown, as well as with those of your bridesmaids and moms. Every woman in a great dress needs to have a stylish wrap or jacket to keep the cold at bay and still look amazing after-hours. And wraps provide an added benefit: some houses of worship don't allow women to show bare arms or shoulders, so those wraps become everyone's official wardrobe for the ceremony hour. All covered up, you're adhering to the rules of the house. The big mistake here is in *not* having the matching wraps to depend on during the ceremony, and not encouraging the ladies to bring a jacket, pashmina, or shawl to the wedding. Especially at yacht and beachfront weddings, it can get quite cold. Yes, we all love the chivalry of a man giving us his jacket to wear, but why should he freeze, and why should you look lost in his big, broad-shouldered suit jacket?

DO: Send out an e-mail to the bridesmaids, letting them know about a coordinating style of pashmina or wrap that you saw on sale at a department store, and ask if anyone wishes for you to pick one up for her. Or, make the jackets or pashminas your choice of useful and use-again gifts for your bridesmaids. You'll ensure that they'll look great, and they'll love the luxurious gift you chose for them. With the average bridesmaid gift reaching the $75 mark, this is infinitely doable on this budget.

DON'T: Forget the moms and child attendants, including junior bridesmaids, plus grandmothers, aunts, and friends. This is definitely a topic to bring up with the ladies on your list—tell them that it gets chilly by the lake at night, so make sure you bring along a light jacket. Guests love it when they hear you're looking out for them, so consider adding this wardrobe suggestion to your personalized wedding website!

149. Not making plans for air conditioning— or heat—for everyone's comfort ⊗⊗⊗

It's a huge mistake to try to save a few bucks by not renting the air conditioners or heating units your site manager or wedding coordinator suggested. Yes, they cost a few hundred each, but you can't put a dollar sign on your wedding tent being warm and cozy against the damp chill of an October night. Tempting fate, and Mother Nature, with your guests' comfort on an issue as unpredictable as the temperature and dampness or humidity is gambling with the overall success of your wedding. You could have the dream menu from heaven or a cake that's headed right for the cover of a bridal magazine, but if all of your guests froze their butts off, or steamed in the hot sun without the simple amenity of air conditioning, your wedding becomes a tale of wasted time and energy by those guests whose standards are high and whose lips are loose with gossip. And even if you don't care about what others think, surely you must care about keeping grandma comfortable, having fans for those guests who are pregnant, not having guests faint from the heat, and seeing flowergirls' teeth chattering. Invest in portable heat or cool air, and some couples in tropical climates or whose weddings are in the busy summer season of more than 100 degrees have been known to rent misters for a quick dash through a cooling spray. They bring your guests relief, and they make for great photos. And I can tell you that the portable heaters are now like tall lampposts with bases that radiate warmth. There's no noise, no blowing of hot wind . . .

just a cozy and comfortable heat emanating from that light post, and don't all of those guests look like they're having a great time sitting right next to that stylish lamppost-heater? Function is the order of the day, but you need to know—to avoid a big mistake—that rented heaters or cooling fans are quite attractive now. Pay up. It's worth it.

It's a huge mistake to try to save a few bucks by not renting the air conditioners or heating units your site manager or wedding coordinator suggested.

150. Going with the cheap portable restrooms ⊘⊘⊘

When your outdoor beach or park wedding location doesn't offer sufficient restroom facilities, you will need to secure portable restrooms for your guests. Now keep in mind that rental agencies offer a range of different styles in different price ranges. There's the boxy industrial porta-potty you see at construction sites and rest stops on desert highways—obviously, that's not your best option for a wedding! And that's exactly the mistake that some brides and grooms make when they're trying to save money or when they book without fully researching their options. This isn't an area where you should take shortcuts! If you think about the elegantly appointed restrooms in hotels and restaurants—with marble counters and spotless mirrors, flattering lighting and clean floors—the formality of the restroom needs to match the formality of your event. So look into renting the higher-level of portable restrooms, many of which reside inside upscale RVs and feature mood lighting, sound systems and a dedicated restroom attendant who keeps track of cleanliness and toilet paper supply. Yes, this costs more, but considering that guests will spend time in the restroom area, it shouldn't be a space that frightens or repulses them. After all that planning for your gorgeous wedding, you don't want guests walking away talking only about the "disgusting bathroom" or feeling like they are at a rest stop on the highway. It's a major mistake not to take great interest in the quality, appearance, and functionality of portable restroom facilities. Remember, you will need to visit them as well . . . in your gown.

DO: Research the wide variety of portable restroom facilities and setups, knowing that you can rent a larger portable restroom without the upscale RV, and just surround it with a separate rented tent, flowers, a vanity table, and great lighting that you arrange. See what your wedding coordinator has done with this common need at weddings; ask to see his or her portfolio focusing on the design of restroom areas. You'll even get inspiration from the coordinator's or floral designer's work in non-portable restrooms, so take notes on lighting, floral arrangements, convenience trays that contain breath mints and hand wipes, and so on.

DON'T: Book anything without seeing it first, and don't take an assurance by a site that they take care of the restroom placement and details as a release from your responsibilities to see them, try them out, and speak up about where you want the restrooms located. True, the site has experience in these matters, but this is your wedding. If you feel that guests won't want to stand in line for portable restrooms in view of the other guests—which is a big tactical error and a source of embarrassment to guests—ask that the portable restrooms be located on the other side of the building, through the garden, or behind a privacy wall that you have your designer construct. Another huge mistake when it comes to restrooms: running out of toilet paper. If you're arranging your own site without the help of a site manager or coordinator, get twice as much toilet paper as you need, stock the rolls in a pretty basket that becomes part of the décor, and also double up on guest hand towels of the paper variety. And don't be afraid to tell the site manager or wedding coordinator that the restroom needs to be straightened up during the reception . . . great wedding hosts pop into the facilities to look for messes and supplies running low, and they ask for attention to the area often throughout the night.

CHAPTER 20

BONUS CHAPTER! MISTAKES TO AVOID DURING THE CELEBRATION

*Y*ou might think that once your wedding day arrives, your ceremony is over, and you're enjoying your reception, that there's not another mistake to fear. But there are a few missteps to avoid. Many bridal couples cover ever detail perfectly all through the planning, confirming everything with their experts, and then they make a major flub right in the middle of their big day. And *that's* what guests remember. Don't make a last-minute error. Pay attention to the following important warnings, which we've included here as five *free bonus entries!*

1. Not circulating to greet guests ◌◌◌

It may be hard to imagine, but some brides and grooms never make it a point to visit each table to greet their guests! When the first dance is over, they either head right to the bar to join their friends, stay on the dance floor, or just sit at the sweetheart table in their own little world. Guests, then, have to come to *them* to offer their congratulations and those cash wedding gift envelopes, which often elicits grumbles of "oh, we have to come to *you*" from some guests who see the couple's lack of circulating as a form of arrogance. Don't be rude. Visit with your guests.

DO: Plan to visit each guest table as soon as humanly possible. The best brides and grooms do so right after the first dances and before the meal is served. This shows their deep appreciation for their guests' presence and efforts in getting to the wedding. They care so much about their guests that they want to speak with them right away. I attended a wedding recently where the bride and groom circulated to each guest table right at the start of the reception, and then they came around *again* before the cake was cut ... just to get quality time with their friends, family, and colleagues. That was a marvelous class act, one that all the guests noticed and discussed. Even better, the *parents* of the bride and groom took the time to circulate to each table, even to tables of the other side's guests, to shake hands, exchange hugs, and accept compliments on the lovely celebration. That too is a definite do.

DON'T: Think that you're intruding on guests' conversations or that you're only visiting tables to accept those cash gift envelopes. Believe it or not, some guests actually *want* you to come get that envelope right away. It makes them nervous to hold on to the envelope because they don't want to lose it while dancing.

Don't be rude. Visit with your guests.

2. Taking on problems that arise during the day ⊘⊘⊘

You're the guests of honor! What are you doing in the kitchen telling the site manager that the servers aren't making enough rounds with the hors d'oeuvres? Why are you trying to find someone to go get more ice? There's an entire staff at the wedding site that is prepared to handle the little things that go wrong, if not a wedding coordinator who has a team of assistants to handle that serving issue, or the fallen flower arch, the party crashers, or the drunk guest who needs to be removed. And even if you've self-hosted the wedding at a site where there is no manager or coordinator, you should designate a team of assistants who will handle the little things, like running out to buy more ice, so that you can continue to enjoy your party uninterrupted. Things go wrong at weddings, and staff and volunteers often do a great job of keeping these things hidden from the bride and groom. Experts are well trained in every possible scenario, so they know the right diplomatic wording to ask a drunk guest to have a cup of coffee, and they have full sheet cakes in their refrigerators in case a layer of your cake falls to the floor (it has happened). If any guest comes to you with a problem, it's perfectly okay for you to escort them to the site manager, explain the need, and then with a smile rejoin your party. For larger problems, parents can step in to help form a replacement plan.

DO: Consider hiring a wedding coordinator just for day-of-wedding assistance, to handle everything from organizing delivery of items, overseeing setup, sending assistants out to buy more supplies, and miraculously solving problems right there on the spot. It doesn't cost a lot, and is in fact a form of wedding insurance. Visit *www.bridalassn.com* to find an accredited wedding coordinator near you, and ask about the time commitment needed for prewedding meetings and the sharing of your detailed itinerary. You'll be happy you have an expert on your side, so that all the problems don't fall on your shoulders.

DON'T: Overobligate your bridal party as worker bees on your wedding day. They're your attendants, not your employees, so it's never okay to tell them they can't drink because you may need them to go out and buy more liquor or more food, drive home a drunk guest (there are taxis for that), or field questions from your vendors. It *is* okay to ask your maid of honor and best man for one or two favors during the night, such as stepping in to rescue a friend from an overly flirtatious cousin.

3. Not making a toast to all who helped ⊗⊗⊗

We're no longer in an age where the only toasts at the wedding are given by the best man and then the maid of honor. Brides and grooms are taking the microphone and proposing toasts to each other, and to their parents for helping to create such a wonderful wedding celebration. It's a mistake to stay silent and let everyone else do the talking. Your friends and family have traveled a long way to attend your wedding. Thank them in a toast to all. Your site manager and staff, the chef, the baker, the disc jockey, and all the other experts who are working *through* the party to make sure everything is perfect deserve a round of applause, so it's a wonderful, gracious offering if you add in a separate toast to them as well. Guests *love* seeing brides and grooms who extend their gratitude to those who have delivered everything they asked for, and are going above and beyond what the couple expected. Your toast doesn't have to be poetry. Just a simple, "we'd like to take a moment to thank [name], our wedding coordinator, and [name], our caterer, plus their amazing staff members, for bringing our wedding vision to life so beautifully. Cheers to you!" Not taking time to thank *anyone* is now seen as an all-about-me mentality, which is one of the biggest mistakes you can make on the wedding day.

YOUR TOAST LIST
Write down the names of all the people you'd like to recognize in toasts at your rehearsal dinner and at the wedding, so that you don't make the grievous error of leaving anyone out. You don't get a do-over on this one!

_____

_____

_____

_____

_____

_____

_____

_____

4. Getting drunk and not behaving with class ⊘⊘⊘

By virtue of your being the bride and groom, the spotlight is on you in a room full of family members and colleagues, and representatives of your families. Your behavior speaks volumes to all. So that means taking it easy with the alcohol. Yes, this is a celebration and the wine (and martinis) will flow, but if you're slurring your words or getting sick in the bathroom, that qualifies as a wedding disaster. Tipsy is okay, trashed is not okay . . . even if your social group regularly goes clubbing and being inebriated is an accepted state in your circle of friends. On this important day, you'll need to exercise moderation. Because you do want to *remember* your wedding day, and—as videographers say—the camera captures *everything*.

DO: Make sure you have plenty to eat so that you're not drinking on an empty stomach, which could render you dizzy after just one champagne toast. Stick to one kind of mixed drink, since skipping from drink to drink can make you sick. And to stay clearheaded and really present on your day, you might wish to order more soft drinks or water than hard alcohol concoctions.

DON'T: Be afraid to ask your groom to put down the mixed drinks as well. Surely he will want to be lucid on the wedding day . . . and night.

5. Not enjoying the food! ◌◌◌

The reception flies by in a flash, and if you don't make a concerted effort to stop, sit down, claim your own time to eat, and enjoy the selection at the buffet table, your entrée, and your cake, you'll wind up like so many other brides and grooms who complain, "I didn't even get to taste the food!" So much care and thought went into choosing each delectable dish, it would be a shame if you—the guests of honor—not only missed out on the menu, but heard from *everyone* how terrific everything was.

DO: Make it your plan—you'll each fix yourselves a heaping plate of food from the cocktail party, and you'll steal away to a private room upstairs or on the grounds, where you can enjoy your platter quickly and add some romance by feeding each other those tasty morel mushrooms or shrimp and mango skewers. Inform the maitre d' that you'd like to be informed when your dinners are placed at your sweetheart table, and then lead your new spouse over to dig into your entrées. Ask that the first slices of cake be left at your place settings, not whisked away from you when they wheel the cake into the kitchen. It's okay if you eat your cake first! You have to make it a rule that you'll enjoy your full menu, even if it means leaving the actual celebration for fifteen minutes to eat in peace.

DON'T: Depend on friends you've asked to bring you some food. In the excitement of the celebration, they too get caught up in mingling, and they may not deliver a hot plate when they see that you're chatting with friends as well. This plan often backfires, even if it's the staff who promised to bring platters out to the bridal party while you're posing for photos. You'll probably miss out on those treats as well, since so many snapshots need to be taken. Your goal, the ultimate goal, is to enjoy every minute of your beautiful wedding, and have no regrets about avoidable mistakes.

NOTE FROM THE AUTHOR

*Y*ou're now in great shape to avoid the most common wedding mistakes, those blunders you'd otherwise hate yourself for committing, which can have drastic, negative effects on your wedding day *and* the people around you.

While no one ever *intends* to make a big mistake when it comes to a wedding, details get lost in the shuffle, emotions are running high, and miscommunications abound. In short, the state you're going to be in all through the wedding-planning stage is bound to allow a few mistakes to get through. So promise yourself now that you'll keep your sense of humor as well as a deep sense of confidence in yourself that you can handle whatever arises. Some things happen on wedding days that no one could ever have predicted, and you can't avoid every mishap.

And some mistakes leads to even better results. For example, if you've forgotten to give the pianist the list of songs you want for the ceremony, he might perform songs you've never heard before ... songs that are absolutely beautiful, way better than those cliché classical numbers you wanted, and that become a lasting part of your love story. Sometimes the mistakes we make can lead to bigger and better things....

Again, I encourage you to share this book with your bridal party members, parents, and groom so that they too can avoid some of the mistakes in the wedding minefield, or so that they can gently remind *you* of these insights if you seem to have forgotten a few of them. Better to have your team prepared with these insider secrets for the ultimate good of your wedding and your happiness.

If you would like to contribute your suggestions for a future edition of this book, with all new wedding mistakes to avoid, please visit me at *www.sharonnaylor.net* and share your stories. I may include your tale for the benefit of future brides and grooms who *you* can help save from mistakes that can wreck their big days.

Thank you for allowing me to be a part of your wedding preparations!

Sharon Naylor

THE TOP TEN BRIDAL PARTY MISTAKES

As a bridal party member, you already have a lot to keep track of—the deadlines for sending in payments and measurements, the dates of prewedding parties, how you're going to deliver the reading during the ceremony—but there are a few additional important things to keep in mind: you must avoid the top ten bridal party mistakes! Here they are for your fair warning:

1. **Not paying on time.** Ugh! This one twists the bride into a knot, since waiting for a bridal party member to send a check, or having to pay a rush fee for gown or tux delivery, will destroy the wedding couple's peace of mind. Don't be the troublemaker. Pay early. As soon as they let you know the amount.

2. **Not showing up for shopping trips.** You said you could attend, but something came up at the last minute. You might think it would be okay for the bride to just send you a link for the dress she likes, but she really wants you there in person. So don't flake.

3. **Wanting to be the boss.** Regardless of which role you've been given, when you get aggressive and want to win the alpha role in the group, you're just going to annoy everyone and inspire a mutiny. Let the bride and groom be in charge, and the bridal party just delivers what's asked of them.

4. **Complaining about money after the fact.** If the bride asks you, "is this dress outside of your price range?" say yes if it is. It does no good to agree to a dress in an upper echelon price range and then complain about the price to anyone who will listen.

5. **Not suggesting ideas.** When the bride gathers you for a brainstorming session over lunch, or a meeting with the florist, have something to say. Brides hate it when they go to great lengths to include everyone in the planning, and then everyone gets meek and super-agreeable at the actual meeting. Speak up!

6. **Entering into group games.** The younger and more immature members will join into cliques and set themselves apart from other members of the bridal party as a matter of human nature in a social and hierarchical setting, so don't allow or entertain any bad group dynamics, gossip, fights, or power struggles. Be a unified team for the bride and groom's sake.

7. **Being an etiquette hound.** You may think you know the best and most proper ways to do everything, according to an etiquette book you read, but the bride and groom don't need

you to correct them. It's actually the trend for couples to bend traditional etiquette to allow them the personalized wedding day they want.

8. **Joking about causing trouble on the wedding day.** You're close to the couple, you know the bride is on edge about things going wrong, so what harm can it do to joke about bringing the groom's ex-girlfriend as your date to the wedding? Lots. Skip the teasing and the jokes, understanding that the bride and groom have a lot riding on this wedding day, so the usual level of joking and pranks isn't welcome right now. Keep the teasing to a minimum, and declare the bride off-limits for your entire group's humor attacks.

9. **Getting drunk at the wedding.** Tipsy is okay. Hitting on the bride's parents or siblings is not okay.

10. **Making a vastly inappropriate wedding toast.** Again, the bride is off-limits for off-color teasing, and the groom's past sex life is off-limits as well. You'll be in a room filled with the couple's friends and relatives, colleagues, and bosses, so don't be so narrow-minded as to think that frat-type humor is going to go over well. You'll just embarrass everyone, and the bride and groom will be extremely upset with you. Study up on good toast-making material and skills (read *Your Special Wedding Toasts* at *www.sharonnaylor.net*) to design the perfect short and sweet toast that will be unforgettable for all the *right* reasons.

THE TOP FIVE ETIQUETTE MISTAKES FOR PARENTS

You might be among the parents who are paying for the entire wedding, or you might be paying for part of the wedding. You might not be paying for anything, but the bride and groom have invited you to participate in the fun of picking out flowers and cakes and looking at venues. Each parent group has its own involvement level these days, but what you all have in common is the need to avoid making the most common etiquette mistakes.

This is a very important time, after all. You're not only helping with the wedding, you're setting the rules for your future relationship with the bride and groom. Mistakes made by parents right now can live on forever in the form of hurt feelings or insult taken at a comment you make to the other side of the family. So be careful to practice good etiquette, keep the bride and groom's wishes above all else, phrase your wishes as requests and not demands, and avoid the top five etiquette mistakes for parents:

1. **Assuming you'll have roles in the wedding.** Weddings are vastly different than they were when you got married, so nothing goes by the old rules that you expect. Don't invite any problems by assuming that you'll get to do x, y, and z because you're the parents of the bride or groom. The couple gets to decide who will do what, even if you're kicking in a percentage of the wedding costs. And even if you're kicking in a large percentage of the costs, it's good etiquette now to let the bride and groom make all the decisions anyway.

2. **Overruling the bride and groom.** They've made their plans, so let them stick to it. One of the top mistakes is giving them the old "we're paying for it" argument when they confront you about how you called the caterer and changed a few things. This is a time of change. So if you've been a hands-on parent even into the bride or groom's adult life, it's time for you to step back and not try to control things.

3. **Speaking badly of the bride, groom, or their family to others.** Even if you're totally frustrated, your words live on forever. So don't vent about how selfish the bride is, or how uninvolved the groom is, or how tacky the bride's mother's ideas are to other people. Word gets around, and these judgments come back to bite you. If you have to vent, do it into a journal instead.

4. **Asking others to give a shower.** You can't ask someone else to give a shower as a way for you to slide underneath the

traditional etiquette rule that parents don't give showers on their own. While it's true that more mothers are co-planning showers with the bridal party, they're asked by the group. You can't obligate an aunt or family friend to throw the shower for them, even though you have good intentions. Just let the maid of honor know that you're willing to chip in and help with whatever's needed.

5. **Inviting too many people.** Parents make a big mistake when the initial engagement gets them inviting all of their friends and colleagues to the wedding. Even if the bride and groom say "it's going to be big," it's still wise to wait for *their* assignment of how many guest spots you get. In weddings of decades ago, the parents who were paying for the wedding also invited a big group of guests of their own, but now with weddings so expensive there's not a lot of room for extra people. Particularly extra people who don't know the bride and groom. So hold back on extending verbal invitations until you get a chance to talk with the bride and groom about the guest list. You'll be an invaluable asset when it comes to figuring out the family members who will be invited, and the more agreeable you are with that phase, the more likely the bride and groom will be to let you invite a few extra friends. What's most important is waiting to hear from them.

THE TOP FIVE MISTAKES IN WEDDING TOASTS

When you take the microphone to make a toast at a wedding, all eyes are on you and everything you say becomes immortalized in the wedding video, not to mention in the minds of everyone there. Not too much pressure, right? We'd like to remind you of the top five etiquette mistakes that are all-too-often made with wedding toasts, because we don't want you to be *that person* who brought the wedding to a screeching halt. You already know that you shouldn't toast while drunk. Here are the other top don'ts:

1. **Don't talk forever.** Long and rambling toasts have no place at a wedding, and when you pass annoying you get to self-centered. Everyone there will think you just want to hear yourself talk. So keep your toasts to the two-minute range, and know ahead of time that you can make toasts at other prewedding parties like showers and bachelor or bachelorette parties, and so on. For the big day, a toast should be short, sweet, and sentimental (and a little bit funny if *you* are).

2. **Telling inappropriate stories.** Yes, we all know the bride and groom have a past, but it's supremely bad form to bring it up either directly or in code now. The bride *will* know what you're talking about when you mention that wild spring break. Keep the focus on the here and now. The raunchy stuff has no place at a wedding.

3. **Using off-color language.** Not only are there kids and elders in the room, it just makes you sound classless when you drop off-color language. It may be your natural way of speaking, but clean it up for the day. And know that in some families, their version of a curse word may be different from yours. So even the tame ones should be off limits.

4. **Not mentioning both the bride and groom.** If you're the best man, for instance, you can talk about what a great guy the groom is, but also talk about how much you like the bride and what she's brought into the groom's life. A one-way toast doesn't honor them as a couple, so be sure you talk about both of them.

5. **Poaching the toast.** This is a bad one. If you're at the rehearsal dinner, the parents of the groom make the first toast if they're the hosts. It's a bad, bad breach of etiquette to steal their spotlight and act like it's your party. Wait for the host to make his or her speech, then the couple makes a toast to thank their bridal party, and then others can speak.

INDEX